Behave Yourself

How to BE yourself and HAVE the life you want

Joanna Infeld

ISBN (13) 978-0-9979047-3-4

K O R A
P R E S S

Published by Kora Press ®
www.KoraPress.com

Contents

Introduction 5

A Ladder of Reasons 9

How to Have an Effective Argument 23

The Stereotypes Gallery 27

Presumption 30

Jealousy 33

To Think Is to Crete 37

Tugging 39

Triggering 43

Value 45

Telling a Secret 51

Waiting 53

Aging 55

Living With Grace 59

Permission 63

Assumption 67

Give and Take 71

Security 75

Change 77

Blame 79

Gain and Loss 85

High and Low Energies 89

Being Clean 93

Colors in the Aura 95

Every Moment Counts 97

Linking and Thinking 99

Points of View 101

Talking About Others 107
Asking for Help 109
Sacred Sites 113
Express and Ingest 115
Homo Erectus 117
The Sacred Is Everywhere 119
Change Your Vibration 121
Clairvoyance 123
Talent 127
The Knife Story 129
Connection Is Possible 133

Introduction

The study of human behavior is a fascinating subject, forever changing, developing, metamorphosing as humans themselves learn, grow, change and adopt new reasons for doing what they do or adapt to transforming social, cultural and political conditions. We are forever evolving, and our behavior reflects this trend by giving rise to new habits, customs, mores, ceremonies and traditions all the time. That is why this study is so interesting. Human behavior combines universal and perpetual traits as well as those forged by a nation, a people, a community, a locality, or those developed at a particular time and circumstance in history.

The sketches in this book have been selected randomly and do not assume to be exhaustive by any means. They are merely observations based on experience and a few simple technologies collected from years of working with people who have undertaken a study of themselves, of the times we live in, and of human nature and behavior in many ordinary and extraordinary situations.

The one thing that sets this study apart from a manual on human behavior and customs is the fact that it is an attempt to overlay two studies: one is the study of human nature, and the other is an understanding and sensitivity to the unseen worlds and the human energy field. It is largely accepted today that all humans have an aura and that we radiate electric impulses throughout our bodies, brains, muscles, and internal organs, including our heart. Ever since conception we are surrounded by this energy field which is initially confined to the womb, but at birth it expands and precedes us into the birth canal. Anyone who has ever accompanied a mother in labor will know the special feeling that attends the miracle of birth. And so, as we grow older, our electromagnetic field expands as well, making us occupy spaces larger than our physical bodies. When we enter a room, our aura is there before us; when we sit in a chair or stand talking to someone, we register the energy field of another person before we exchange a glance or even know consciously that they are approaching. This is why we can often feel someone entering our energy field, even if we do not see them.

How many times have you turned around, to find someone standing behind you, or perhaps even just looking at you from a distance? Eyes, having a direct connection to the brain, and being the only examples of live tissue that we can see when we look at another human being, carry and transfer energy in a very powerful way. How many times have you felt someone's look which has changed your energetic state, by making you feel any of a whole myriad of emotions, like embarrassment, shame, guilt, excitement—sexual or otherwise—happiness, curiosity, or pity?

Your aura is as much a part of you as your physical body. With practice anyone can learn to see, feel, and ultimately heal the human energy field. Most diseases start in the unseen and slowly move inside the human, manifesting eventually in the seen and medically documented aspects of the human design. That is why many diseases have a long incubation period—they first have to work their way into the physical body before the recognizable symptoms will appear. However, as soon as the virus or bacteria are inside the aura, they can begin to affect the person without any diagnosable symptoms appearing on the screens of computers belonging to medical laboratories and doctors' offices. A skilled medical clairvoyant or energy practitioner (and there are many who are not so good, as well as many charlatans and imposters) might be able to sense the invasion within the aura and actually take it away, using his or her hands to do so, before it finds its way into the physical body.

These are new sciences, as well as the oldest in the world. The new revival of these understandings has been a long time coming, and we are on the brink of a time when there will need to be electromagnetic doctors who, with the tools of their trained and sensitive hands, their open minds, and vast experiences in these realms, will be able to diagnose and cure the diseases of tomorrow, which more and more will be electrically based. These maladies will be stemming from incorrect ways of thinking, from lack of purpose, intention and will; in other words, they will originate within the energy field of a person and will reside there, as long as the environment promulgated by the patient allows them to do so.

We are approaching fascinating times of change, and the human evolution is guiding us toward a situation within which a greater fraction of our brains will open up to conscious thought patterns, introduced by those who have disciplined themselves to train their faculties to explore these new territories. We still have a long way to go, but where is it written that a long way cannot be traversed in a comparatively short time?

A Ladder of Reasons

Thee are many reasons why people do what they do, and there are many levels of reasons, which make a person's subsequent actions more or less effective and more or less powerful. This writing will be divided into three parts: the first will examine personal reasons, the second will look at collective or community reasons, and the third is entitled *A Ladder of Reasons*—it will demonstrate how there are many reasons why a person will do something and how different reasons are connected to different levels of power.

Part One: Personal Reasons
The first thing to say about reasons is that they are connected to power, so the stronger the reason for something, the more the power. To give a personal example: if somebody had said to me, "Go to a stranger's house and ask for a glass of water so that I can have a drink," I probably wouldn't do it. But on one occasion my friend was looking at his car which was parked in front of an apartment block, trying to work out why it wouldn't go, and in his attempt to check out what was wrong, he started to clean off the battery and splattered some acid into his eyes. He fell to the ground, crying in pain. I didn't know anybody in the district, but I just ran into the nearest building and knocked on several doors that I could access, shouting and begging for water. The

reason was that I wanted to help alleviate my friend's pain, or perhaps even help prevent him from going blind. So because of this powerful reason, I did something that I would never have done for a lesser reason. Just to conclude the story, someone did give me a glass of water, the paramedics soon arrived, and my friend was fine by the next day.

If a person does something to save one's life or the lives of one's loved ones, then that is a very powerful reason and it will propel even a shy person into extraordinary, courageous and bold acts. There are many, many stories, from the time of war, for example, when people would risk their lives to help another. And it wouldn't necessarily be someone whom you would expect of being a hero. Very often the person who jumps into a lake to save a child is just a neighbor, but finding themselves in that circumstance, something great can rise in them and to them it is the most natural thing to do. "I am no hero," they usually say after the fact, "anybody would do what I have done." To help another and save a life is a powerful reason. If there is a fire, even a very shy person will go into a crowded room and shout "Fire," because they know that by doing so they can save a number of people's lives. So that is a very powerful reason indeed.

Depending on the reason, you can choose to do things or decide not to, and that is why it is important to have the right reasons for doing what is important to you, so that you can connect to the power that will guarantee success. The more powerful and elevated the reason, the more effective the action and the more sustainability and longevity it may have. So, for example, if you decide to learn Spanish on a whim because you think it is cool to speak another language, then you will probably not continue the lessons for very long. If you go to class because your friend is going, you might carry on as long as the friend keeps going, which means that you are depending on someone else's will, not your own. So the moment it becomes a little bit difficult, you will probably drift away. That happens a lot, when people sign up to learn something new following their New Year's resolutions or when the academic year begins. If they haven't got powerful enough reasons to continue, they are usually gone by Christmas. However, if you have a more powerful reason—let's say, for example, you've been offered a job somewhere in Spain or South America, and it's a good job, and your livelihood depends on it, and one of the conditions of the job is that you learn Spanish, then all the more chances that you will see it through and that you will have more energy to sustain that endeavor.

The more constant and repetitive the action and the stronger the reasons, then the more chances you have of being successful and fulfilling your intentions. For every action there is an opposite and equal reaction. Everything you do, everything you think, causes something—it releases a little bit of energy into the atmosphere of the planet and stays there, because energy cannot be destroyed. So if you do an action once, it has a limited effect. But if you keep doing it, in the end, the very fact of your having done it repetitively will change you and it will also influence your surroundings, and the atmosphere of the district. So, for example, if you do decide to learn Spanish and you go to the language school, say, twice a week, for months, in the end, you will learn the new language. And you don't even have to be very good at languages, because persistence and repetition work wonders. If you observe a plant, it doesn't grow in one big effort; it grows by many, many, many small efforts. But in the end it will push through the earth, or even concrete and come into the light.

Here is another example. Let's take the repetitive action of going to work every day, which most of us do. Well, there are many reasons why you might want to go to work, and an obvious one is to make a living. That singular reason certainly has a power attached to it and it will cause you to get up in the morning, arrive punctually and make sure that you don't get fired. But it only goes so far and it certainly will not necessarily bring satisfaction to the job. Because if the only reason for going to work is to make a living, you might end up being resentful and not enjoying what you do, and getting up in the morning with a certain reluctance, and even a grudge. Because the only way to go to work, and enjoy it, and to be grateful for the fact that you have a job, is to really love what you are doing. That is a more powerful reason, because if you go to work because you enjoy it, and you derive satisfaction from it, then you certainly will have a greater incentive to get up the morning and get in the car, or take the bus, or subway, and go to work. There can be even greater reasons, because you might have a job that not only gives you satisfaction, but gives other people satisfaction as well. Maybe you work for a charity, and you help other people, and you enjoy it, and you make a living as well. Well, then you have many reasons with much more power attached to them. Then you can go even further—you might be an artist who also derives inspiration and revelation from what you do, and you are making a living, and it can be helping others if you are donating part of your income to charity, or you are teaching others how to execute your craft. So you can have many reasons in one action, and the much more powerful way to go on is to have many reasons for a single action, rather than the other way round, which is—to do many actions for one reason.

To conclude the first part of this writing, I suggest that you sit down with pen and paper and write down your reasons for doing what you do, especially such repetitive actions as going to work. If you are finding that some routine tasks are difficult to perform, you might want to find new reasons for doing them, thereby increasing the power with which you do them.

Exercise:
Answer the following questions:
Why do I work?
Why do I get up in the morning?
Why do I live where I live?

Part Two: Collective Reasons
Let's look for a moment at the idea of ceremony and customs. Many traditions stem from an ancient understanding concerning the natural worlds of energy. Mostly ancient people devised ceremonies and rituals that would produce a desired energetic effect into the community. But very often the initial reasons for these ancient celebrations get lost and centuries later people might carry on performing the actions, but they don't necessarily understand why. And that's why you can ask those who conduct tribal, religious, or official ceremonies,

"Why do you do this action?" or "Why do you wear that hat, or that costume?" and you will often get an answer, and they will say, "It's tradition." What that means is that somebody somewhere at some point in history knew what they were doing, and did it for a specific reason, but the reason can get lost, and that's when the power gets lost as well, because if people do something, not understanding why they are doing it, they won't be able to invest a lot of power into their action, and they won't be able to dedicate a lot of their energy to that ceremony, so then it gets weakened over the years. Then the younger generation grows up and as they participate in these ceremonies, they will wonder, "Why are we doing this?" So consequently they often will stop doing it or they will change the ceremony to adapt it to the customs of the modern times. There is a scene in the film *Fiddler on the Roof* during a wedding ceremony in which the men are dancing separately to the women. A young man asks, "Why is there this separation? Let's bring the men and women together." So he takes down the barrier that had separated them, and both genders start dancing together, which for that generation made total sense and was much more reasonable and enjoyable. But what the young man and the other participants didn't understand is that there originally was a reason for the separation, initiated a long time ago, but it got lost somewhere along the way.

One other aspect to look at in this is that when a group of people do something, it carries more power than if just one person does it. So even if you don't know why you are doing something, but there is a whole group doing it, then this will often cause group conformity, whereby it is difficult for a person to break away from that tradition, because simply the majority says so, that this is how you do it, and mostly everybody conforms, at least for a while. A tradition might continue until there comes a point when it weakens through ignorance, and because people no longer remember the reasons it was initiated in the first place. Then somebody will inevitably break that silence, a bit like in the story of the emperor's new clothes, when the child says, "But he's naked," and then everybody agrees and all are totally relieved that the truth can now be told.

Let's say there is a tribal religion and people establish a way of going on, and they create certain ceremonies throughout the year, and let's say that they understand the forces of nature and they have devised ways to celebrate the spring, and the first appearance of growth. So they create a dance because they feel the changes in nature and want to express the new energy, and celebrate the turn of the seasons. And then years go by and then perhaps even the climate might change, and spring might start earlier, say in April instead of May. But they're still doing their dance and their celebration in May, when really the forces of nature had burst forth in April. It often happens like this, that something changes, and the energy or the force that people had been working with is no longer there, but they continue their traditions, because that's what they are accustomed to. So the ceremony becomes much less effective, because if they were supported by the forces of nature but these are now gone, then the ceremony loses its validity. And yet, it still gets carried on by groups of people, and it still has a certain potency, but it loses the power that goes with the reasons why the people used to do it in the first place.

Part Three: A Ladder of Reasons

Imagine a ladder with seven rungs, and each rung represents a different level of reasons why people do what they do. So, for example, if someone makes an action out of generosity, then that reason will live at the level at which the energy associated with generosity lives. By doing that action they will be adding to the supply of generosity in the world, because like goes to like. The power at each rung of the ladder refines and increases, so that different reasons connect to different levels of power.

And now, to conclude this writing, we will look at seven levels of reasons. These seven levels could be divided into further levels, but for the sake of this writing, we are going to limit it to seven.

Level 7

So we're going to start with the lowest of all which is level seven. The reasons that belong here are revenge, guilt, or wanting to get one's own back. These reasons add to those aggregates of energy, or those essences in the world that are defined by such epithets as greed, aggression, dominance, cruelty, revenge and so on. One of the reasons that there are so many wars in the world is the fact that these collections of power, or banks of force, have been added to throughout history, especially during the last two centuries. So the energy is still there, it has not been destroyed, it has not been equalled out; therefore for any nation or person to connect to aggression is easy, because there is a lot of it about, and the more of it gets added to, the easier it will be for other people to connect to it as well. So if you want to be somebody who is working to invalidate these negative energies, then there is more a call upon you to add to the essences that are high that can equal out and superimpose themselves upon the lower powers. To counterbalance aggression and cruelty, for example, one would need to work for peace and compassion.

Level 6
So moving quickly along, at the next level, the next rung of the ladder, which is level six, there is gain and prevention of loss, habit and tradition. This is where people will go to work to make a living. It is also the level of maintenance—keeping going, trying to have a life that has no bother in it, no trouble, but also no inspiration, no higher ideals. Level six is also the daily grind, the daily life, everything we do habitually, with not much thought attached to it, and not many reasons, just really trying to continue living—that belongs at level six. It goes with boredom, not wondering why one is alive here on this planet, just trying to survive.

Level 5
At level five there are such reasons like wanting to learn, wanting to improve, wanting to refine, wanting to progress. So all the libraries and universities of the world start at this level and if you do something to improve yourself, you are automatically lifting yourself out from the level of maintenance to something a little bit more elevated, a little bit more progressive, and a little bit more powerful. It must be said that sometimes people go to college or university for reasons other than self-improvement. So if they attend college for self-gain and for economic reasons only, then they are still based in

level six, even though they are learning and educating themselves in the process, and attending a place where level five can be connected to.

Level 4
Level four is about doing something for unselfish reasons and doing something with a bigger view, for example, for the family, for for a group, for the nation, or even for the whole human race. The bigger the reason, the more power will be associated with it. Multiplicity wields power, both for good and for bad. So if many people adhere to a belief or perpetuate a custom, it will in time gain power. At level four, if someone does something to add to the essence of care, or patience, or understanding in the world, then that quality will attend them and help them in return. So there is support from the existing powers associated with individual qualities that will come and enhance the reasons why a person does what they do, if they can reach level four.

Many tribal customs with which groups of people have connected to the forces of nature derive from this level. Trying to connect to this level is a very rewarding and courageous thing to do, because there is a shortage of level four in the world; it is much cleaner than the lower levels. So when you lift yourself up to this level, and you do something in an unselfish way to benefit others, and to help the world become a better place, then automatically you put yourself in a space where you can feel very clean about what you do. It is very unlike levels six and seven (especially seven where if you do something for a reason that lives at this level, you can only feel dirty and polluted). Your conscience will guide you and let you know instinctively at which level you reside. We all vacillate between levels and we do things for many reasons. So one moment we might be doing something to improve ourselves, and the next moment we might be cooking ourselves dinner for no other reason than because we want something to eat to sate our hunger. So it varies, and within a day, you probably will go through three or four levels. But if you listen to yourself and listen to your instincts, then you will learn to detect which level you are at, because each level feels very different from all the other levels. It is comparatively easy to lift oneself up from one level to the next level above it—just review and adjust the reasons why you do what you do.

Level 3
This is where new knowledge enters the picture—not the kind of new knowledge you get at universities, though originally universities were there to connect to the universe, as the name suggests. New knowledge is to do with the energies and forces of nature that are alive and with us today, just as they have always been. They are regenerative, forever appearing anew and periodically being energetically refreshed. These levels are connected to human purpose and the understanding why humans are here on planet Earth, and to the fact that there is a reason and a mission associated with every human life.

Levels 2, 1
The urge to live is a powerful reason and it carries with it an energy that is mostly hidden, because for most people there is no call for it to manifest on a day to day basis. So it might appear to be absent, but it does live within

each one of us at an automatic level—it is written into our design. So if your life has ever been threatened, if your continuance is ay risk—for example, there is a car coming at you at speed, then something automatically switches on and you will jump out of the way, just as a child that reaches and touches a stove that is hot, immediately will draw their hand back. That is the automatic system. So wanting to continue to live is a great spur and motivation. For example, if someone in a family becomes ill, or there is danger to a community, then suddenly people will find within themselves great strength and resources to help others. There is an example of a mother being able to actually lift a car if her child is trapped underneath and finding in herself that great strength, which says that it is always there, though usually we cannot tap into it. It is in the reservoir of strength within the body, connected to through the adrenaline system, so that it can switch on in times of emergency. But mostly we do not have access to it.

So if the desire to live becomes more conscious—and this is where the work of development really begins—and the person adds up that yes, they want to live, and yes, that they have good reasons to do so, then this extraordinary power can become available to serve their deeper purpose that lies within the longing for continuance and longevity. Why do you want to live? is an essential question to answer, if you wish to connect to higher levels of energy. Even if you come to the answer today, you might want to relook at this question many times over, because as you move along on this journey of development, you will find deeper and deeper reasons with more and more power, just to keep you going. And the more power is available to you, the better the journey will become. So I will end this chapter with that one question again—Why do you want to live?

Exercise
Write down your answer to this question:
Why do I want to live?

How to Have an Effective Argument

In any relationship, within which there is an exchange of energies, there are bound to be times when it is necessary to argue something out. With two people representing two different histories, two different points of view, and two different belief systems, there will be times when it is necessary to find common ground. The important thing is to argue-stretch, rather than argue with heat.

Arguments can be caused by lack of communication, or by the coming together of different frequencies and speeds. There might be the clashing of opposing needs, or two different ways of thinking about a person or an event. Arguments call for explanation and understanding; it is important to hear the other person out so that you understand where they are coming from and why they do what they do.

Arguments are mostly sparked off by actions, not thoughts. They happen when the end result of a thinking (or emotional) process manifests itself. This means that the process which has led to the offending action had begun earlier, but the thinking behind the action can only be argued about when the physical manifestation occurs.

Prevention is better than a cure. Sometimes small, innocent actions that might seem a little "off" lead to larger offenses that initiate more serious arguments later.

That is why it is useful to question behavior that seems a little off or odd, before it precipitates a full-blown argument. It is inevitable that differences in frequency will occur in intimate relationships, and they will not go away if you choose to ignore them. When two or more people come together, they bring with them their ways of thinking, their experiences, and their opinions as to how the relationship (whether personal or professional) should proceed. They can either create great harmony between them, or the clashing of personalities, or both.

A successful argument is aimed at a purpose and is underpinned by value. Its aim is to find resolution to and understanding of a situation, and another person's viewpoint. It clears the air between people and allows for a new beginning. It creates a space for the restatement of the initial contract and can be a herald of a new elevation within a relationship. That is why "making up" can be so emotionally satisfying.

It is important to keep cool when having an argument. If misunderstandings remain unspoken, the underlying frustration can cause a person to get hot until they "can't take it any more," and explode with resentment, while the other person might not even have realized that anything was wrong.

Here are a few tips to have a successful argument:

1. Restate your value

Before beginning, restate your value for each other. Value will provide a larger context within which much can be said without diminishing or jeopardizing the relationship. To be able to accurately state your value for another person, so it comes across as genuine and real, it is important to add it up beforehand. Arguments can sometimes get out of hand, so it is important to add up that you want the relationship to continue.

2. Stay within the subject of the causing incident

Identify the cause of the problem and talk it through— what caused it, how could it have been handled better? When did the trouble start, and could it have been tackled sooner? Do not use an argument as an opportunity to bring in other incidents. Avoid words like, "never," and "always." Argue about one incident at a time.

3. Exhaust the subject

Exhaust the subject and make sure that everything that needed to be said has been said. It might take hours, but it will be worth it, because the problem will not reoccur if you do. Examine all aspects of the situation until you are satisfied that you understand the other person's point of view, even if you do not share it. Place yourself "in their shoes," and let tolerance and understanding rule the day. Another person's anxieties, insecurities, and needs might be different from yours. An argument is an excellent opportunity to learn how another person "ticks."

4. Do not counter-attack

It might be tempting to deflect a criticism that is addressed to you by counter-attacking and finding fault with another person who is explaining why he or she is not happy with you behavior. Do not attack, but listen carefully to what they have to say. Be glad there is someone who cares enough to give you a reflection about yourself.

5. Identify how you feel about the other person's action

If you can identify how the actions of the other person make you feel (disappointed, insecure, angry, etc.), you will be able to easily diffuse the heat that accompanies these emotions. Knowing the correct description of an emotion gives us power over it.

6. Do not walk away

Sometimes you might need a break, and it is fine to take time out from an argument. Do not walk away without explanation in the middle of an argument, because that leaves the other person with the unused energy that was manufactured to see the argument through. If you walk away, you might be giving up the opportunity to resolve your differences.

7. Resolution is achieved by both parties

If you say, "So what do you want me to do?" you are passing on responsibility to the other person. Try to come to a resolution together, so you can both agree how to go forward, or agree to disagree.

The Stereotype Gallery

Throughout our life, most of us form galleries of stereotypes in our mind, fueled by images from literature, films, television, and our own experiences. We have pre-conceived ideas about various professions, races and ages; we attribute a range of behaviors, facial expressions, dress codes, and languages to each of these groups. As soon as a word is mentioned, describing a person as, say a butcher, a picture flashes into our mind and only gets altered if contrary information is received. So if someone is telling a story about a butcher, we might imagine a corpulent middle-aged man with a white apron stained with blood and knife in hand. It can go even further and we might add such details as deep set eyes, a mustache and a balding head; we might add further details, and see that he is narrow minded and a tyrant in his family life. We might see him standing in front of his shop on the high street of a small town.

Other stereotypes might include a hardworking baker, pale as the flour he works with, who gets up when everyone else is still asleep to bake the community's bread. Then there is the spinster teacher with her hair drawn back in a knot, wearing glasses, a grey suit and a blouse with a cameo brooch. Are these characters combinations of qualities we have adopted from movies, and our own memories, or have we met such people on our journey through life?

And what about the policeman, the biker, the accountant, the judge, the hairdresser, the ballet dancer, the pop singer, the absent-minded professor, the talkative bus conductor, or the wild-haired conductor of an orchestra? How many of these would we be able to recognize on the street and how many really do exist?

If we need to play any of these parts in our lives, we can reach for one of the ready-made stereotypes, put it on, like a pair of gloves, and act it out. We are all actors and pretenders, putting on and taking off roles as we see fit. We use them to prevent others from seeing who we really are, because we might feel we are not good enough, educated enough, attractive enough, or knowledgable enough. We tend to pursue the approval of others and validate our existent through external benchmarks. We will go to great lengths to receive confirmation and assurances that we are liked, appreciated, and loved.

Others perceive us through the lens of their own stereotype gallery. If you are accompanied by a younger person, people will assume you are with your son or daughter. People like to define you, just as you like to define the people you meet. It usually starts with questions like, "What do you do for a living?" and "Where are you from?" I have always found this latter question tricky—do people want to know where I was born, where my parents were from, where I grew up, or where I am currently living? To each aspect of this question I would have to provide a different answer.

Some questions are unspoken, but perhaps wondered about, like the age of a person (unless very young or very old), and the status of their bank account. We quickly establish whether we are interested in knowing another person or whether they pose a threat, or whether there is any good energy between us. To make a lasting impression on another person it is important to escape their stereotype gallery and refuse to be boxed in by a single word or phrase. The more original we can be, the longer someone else will remember us.

People have roles for dealing with roles. For example, they will talk differently to a policeman than to their doctor, a potential boss during an interview, or their bridge partner. If they cannot fit you into a role, they might become dislodged from their own role, their mask will slip and you will get a glimpse of the person who lives inside.

Personal development is learning to accept the roleless role, so that one can learn about oneself. We are not a doctor, an editor, or a teacher. We are human beings on a development journey through life. We might have a career and earn a living as a policeman, an actor, or a judge, but what will count in the end is what kind of character we manage to create and what kind of fine qualities we decide to live by.

One way to escape our roles is to adopt and discard new ones all the time. Deliberately placing ourselves in new environments, learning new skills, and meeting new people will help us see ourselves as others see us and learn about our skills and abilities when we are outside our roles.

To help other people show you who they really are, help them ease out of their roles by asking surprise questions, like, "If you were a fruit, what would you be?" or, "What is your finest quality?" For who wants to deal with a stereotype, when the person behind the mask is so much more interesting and has so much more to offer.

Presumption

Presumption and familiarity are close cousins. Presumption is when we fill out the gaps between what we know as facts, and what we do not know, and when we assume we know more than we do. An example is when we meet someone, say for dinner, or at a party, and a third person assumes that we are with our husband, wife, father, mother, son, daughter, sister, or brother, but this is not the case. Another example is when we see the actions of someone and assume we know their motive without checking the facts. Thus we often judge another according to our own criteria without understanding another person's history, reasoning or psychology involved.

How many times have you been given directions to a meeting place, assumed you knew where you were going, only to find out that you had not checked the details. I assume this has happened to you, but perhaps I am mistaken.

We often think we know, when we don't. All our best plans seem to be altered, changed, interfered with, simply because we cannot know it all and there are always unforeseen circumstances that seem to be designed to mess up our precast, carefully arranged movements and plans. Perhaps there is a method in this deviation from our schedules, to ensure that we are not complacent or become too familiar with ourselves, our environment, and other people.

People are unpredictable and we might as well give up trying to forecast what another person will or will not do. We might plan their future, assuming their motivations might be similar to our own, but they have a unique and different perspective on their own life and what they might want for themselves. We can never know the complete genetic makeup of another person, or their history, and their priorities will never be the same as our own. Even in a close relationship, like in a marriage or between mother and daughter, there can never be a sharing of every thought, action and feeling, which is why there will always be surprises in the behavior of others. It is in these gaps between our assumptions and the facts that learning can happen, for taking into consideration the differences between ourselves and others there is an opportunity for exchange and understanding, when we compare our own attitudes with other ways of thinking and being.

Note:
What is the difference between assumption and presumption? The prefix -pre means it occurs beforehand, in the planning stage, whereas assumption is at the point, in the thick of action.

Jealousy

There is a saying, "to be green with envy," and Shakespeare calls jealousy "the green-eyed monster" in *Othello*. Green is the color that appears in the aura when this emotion is present.

Here are four examples of situations in which jealousy can occur and ways to think about them so that this corrosive emotion can be prevented, or, if it is already present, it can be overcome.

Example 1

There is a group of people and they are given a task to perform. When they bring their results together, it appears that one member of the group has performed his or her tasking exceedingly well, in fact much better and faster than anyone else in the group. The other members of the group become jealous and wish it was them who had performed the given task best of all, or that no one else could have done better than they had done. In other words, they either wish that they had done better or that everyone else had done worse. These two possible scenarios would bring about two different results: in the first case, the person would have done better, and the group would have benefitted from their improved performance. In the second scenario, if everyone else would have performed worse, the group result would have been much worse than it already was.

There is a difference between these two scenarios. In the first case the group as a whole would benefit if the jealous members' wishes had come true and everyone would be lifted up to the level of the best performer. Perhaps this kind of envy might encourage the members of the team to improve and to learn from the person who had the best ideas and results. In scenario two, the jealous member of the team wishes everyone else had performed at a level below their ability; if their wish had come true, the entire team would have performed at a much lower level.

So envy is wishing one could have or be something one is not, but jealousy is a desire to win at the cost of others. One way to think about the fact that there is someone who is better than you at a particular skill, or has something that you do not have, is to be glad because there is someone to learn from or something to aspire to. Jealousy, on the other hand, prevents learning and blocks the ability to grow.

Example 2
You were part of a team and you performed a task to the satisfaction of your boss. The boss compliments everyone in the team, praising their work and results, but forgets to mention your name. Do you get upset and wonder, "What about me?" or do you allow your colleagues to have their moment of glory, knowing that you, too, had contributed to their results? If you feel jealous, and express your disappointment, you might spoil the moment for the other members of the team.

Example 3

Someone has something we wish we had—a car, a house, a job, or a trip to an exotic land. We can either wish they did not have it or be glad for their success and work to achieve a similar result. Being glad that someone else has a success and that the essence of success lives in the world means that it is there to be tapped into and to be passed on by contagion. If one person is successful, it paves the way for others to travel along that path as well. Nothing breeds success as well as success. Jealousy, on the other hand, promotes mediocrity and failure.

Example 4

The most common root of jealousy is within a romantic relationship, when one partner puts possession upon the other. When jealousy appears within a relationship, it means that there is either a lack of communication or a lack of commitment. Noone can possess another person. The best way for a relationship to succeed is for both people to have enough resources to be able to leave at any time. That way both partners know that their partner is with them because they want to be. When a person is jealous of another, it means that they are unsure of the other person's commitment to the relationship. It will prevent them from enjoying the opportunity a relationship offers. Jealousy is a sign that a remedy is needed; it usually signals the need for a conversation and honest disclosure of one's feelings, so that the relationship can either be confirmed or dissolved.

To Think Is to Create

It might seem strange that two people going through exactly the same experience can have two very different sensations, reactions, thought processes, and results. This can turn up in such an extreme way that one person might end up elated, while the other becomes depressed; one can be inspired, and the other bewildered; one can be encouraged, and the other disappointed. Thus it is not the external influence that shapes our lives, our health, and moods, but how we think about what happens to us, how we shape our attitudes by our desires, expectations and knowledge.

Looking at the examples mentioned earlier, one person might be excited by meeting a friend for dinner, while another person might not like the person they are due to meet, and wish they could be somewhere else instead. One person might read a book and be inspired by the information contained therein, while another person might not have the education or knowledge to appreciate the subject matter written about within the same book, and end up being frustrated and confused.

One person can live in a self-induced hell inside their own head; to another life is an adventure and a purpose, no matter what anyone else around them thinks or says. It is for each person to design, build, and cultivate the mental edifice of their choosing, within which they then proceed to live, settling in and unpacking their beliefs and thought processes into these self chosen surroundings. Thus one person might live in a palace with many rooms, where each chamber is a new way of thinking and where revelation awaits; another might stubbornly proceed to inhabit only familiar rooms and walk along the same well-chosen paths, thinking the same thoughts for years, or even decades.

There are enough thoughts in the world and universe for every single person to be totally original, fresh, new, and excitingly innovative every single day of their lives. The question is, how many people are daring enough and persistent enough to not give up the first time their expectations are not met, or at the first sign of boredom or weariness?

We create our own reality and then continue to live within that reality. It is developed over years by such influences as upbringing, experience, beliefs, and goals. At any moment we can change our reality by changing our thinking. Thoughts are electrical signals that are as real as the physical worlds that surround us. Even in the most difficult circumstances, we are free to think our own thoughts and create a reality that enhances our lives and shapes our best future.

Tugging

There once was a wise master who had many students. He was starting a new, special group to which he invited, as used to be his way, a few people who had never been part of his group before. When he approached one of these students and asked him if he wanted to be part of the new group, the man replied with a question: "Do you really think I am ready to be part of this group?" "Obviously not," the master replied without missing a beat.

This is an example of tugging. The man in the story was not satisfied with the fact of having been invited to join the group; he wanted to hear further confirmation and thereby draw some more energy from the master to feed his ego and undermine his insecurities. All dealings and exchanges we have with others represent a flow of energy—it passes from us to others and from others to us. If there is a casual conversation, a business call, or a brief encounter, the passage of energy between people will be small. If, on the other hand, we know someone who drains us of energy and seems to suck it out of us, we will learn to avoid such a person at all costs. But sometimes we meet someone who means more to us, and we create a third field of energy between us. We become energetic food for each other as the seeds planted in the third field grow and bear fruits. If we feel that our energy food supply is getting low, and that our self esteem is calling out for a boost, and that our our ego needs confirmation, we will find ways to get more energy, and this is done in many ways. Tugging is one if them.

Everyone thrives on confirmation, and mostly feels they do not get enough of it. The world trades in insecurity and lack of confidence, and to counter-balance this we have developed subtle ways of tugging. Here are a few examples:

"Tell me more,"

"Do you really like it?"

"What else did he say?"

The person saying these words is asking for more energy food. It is not the information contained in the words, but the feeling of being appreciated that we seek.

Sometimes a person might even pretend they have not heard what another is saying to them, just to hear it again, and receive another dose of energy. "I really love you," someone might say. "What is that you said?" their partner asks.

Another example of tugging is making someone ask you to do something twice, by first refusing, while knowing you will comply to their request. Complaint and whining is another example of tugging, aimed at soliciting sympathy or guilt.

"You just go off and enjoy yourself, while I stay here and do all the work."

The person saying these words is really hoping for the opposite effect—they are scheming for the other person to feel guilty, and stay to help them complete their tasks.

Sometimes a person might even make themselves sick, or appear to be sick, just to get attention. This is an extreme example of tugging. A person might even really become sick, because that is their wish and desire.

Someone who hates their job, but loves their hobby, might cause themselves to become ill so they can pursue their passion.

Giving

The opposite of tugging is giving. Have you noticed how when someone gives you something, you soon want to make a return? When you give to another, they will usually want to pay you back in kind. It will have a similar effect to tugging, but it is a win-win situation for both parties. So give to receive. Rather than tugging and demanding, be generous first. Life pays the giver back, perhaps not immediately, and perhaps not from the same person to whom we give, but when you give, you get in return. As the saying goes, "What goes round, comes around."

Surprise your partner, or friend, or family member, and cease the tugging. Practice generosity as a way of life and you might just be amazed how much it can improve your life and increase your energy.

Triggering

Triggering is the higher level beyond tugging and giving. Rather than expecting another person to supply you with energy, and rather than being the donor of energy to another, the way in which both parties immediately receive an energy boost is by triggering.

People who tug at each other have only their own energies to draw upon. But a relationship in which triggering occurs draws energy into the mutually established energy field. In such a relationship both partners connect to higher energies, because they have a mutually agreed purpose.

When tugging, one partner gets energetically fed, while the other supplies the food and loses energy in the interaction between the two partners. However, if an energy transmission is triggered, both partners become enhanced and inspiration can happen to both. To have a higher, selfless purpose, is to surround oneself with an energy field within which higher energetic entities can form up and bring hope and meaning to their hosts.

Value

If you can find value in the little things in life, every moment can become a richness and a joy. "You only get out of life what you put into it" is so true and it is never too late to start putting in more. There is value in being able to feed one's body from day to day, to have the health and strength to walk down the street, to have the time to enjoy a conversation with a friend, or to learn something new.

Question: Why is something valuable?

1. Does rarity cause something to be valuable?
Why are rubies more valuable than pebbles? Is it because they are rare, or because they shine? A rare stamp, even if misprinted, becomes valuable; so does a rare jewel.

How does the planet view rarity? Is the air less valuable because there is an abundance of it and it is free? How would you feel about air if it was taken away?

2. The price tag.
Do people value what they get for free? What if we had to pay for air, language, feelings, emotion, love? Do we save these treasures and use them wisely, or do we squander them without much thought or appreciation? What is the real price of anything?

There are three kinds of payment we can make for

what we get: money, energy and time.

Do you value your body and faculties? If so, which parts? What about those that are unseen or that you don't even know about? How does that value manifest? Are there parts of you that you do not value because you don't like them (for whatever reason)? If we don't like a part of our body, we deprive it of its due appreciation and love, and thereby it is more likely to become diseased.

3. Following the lead.
If everyone else thinks something is valuable, will you follow their lead and assume they are right? How many times have you adopted something into your life, even if you didn't really want it or like it, because others persuaded you or you saw that they thought it was of value? The whole *raison d'être* of fashion is based on the assumption that others know best what to wear and how to wear it.

4. If you lose something, do you value it more?
An obvious example is your health or your freedom, but what about those parts of you that serve you well all the days of your life, like your senses or mind? Will you have to wait until you lose them to value them?

5. Do you value people or things because of what they can do for you?
Or do you value people and things simply because they exist and, like you, are part of Creation?

6. What you cannot do without.
Add up what these things are (for example, your faculties, food, the planet, the laws of nature…) and add up your

value for them. Don't wait until they get taken away or you are in danger of losing them, but build into these aspects of your life a permanent value so that you know where your value lives and you can reach out for it any time, any place, if you need it. For example, contemplate for a moment what it would be like to not be able to sleep or not be able to die, so that you can increase your value for these natural processes.

7. Have a value added life.
Realize that by valuing something you add value to it. When you value something, you send it your power so that it sparkles and shines, and thus can be valued even more. An easy to see example is when you decide you want something that has been in the store for a long time, but you need to come back for it later, because you had not brought your money with you. When you come back you find that someone else had bought what you were hoping to possess. By deciding you wanted it, you had added value to it and made it more attractive to others.

Value what you have and it will become more valuable. If you value your life and existence, they will become more valuable, and others will come to value you more, as well.

8. Are you of value?
Will you be of value to something higher than you? How valuable are you to your family, your community, your country, or to the planet itself?

9. What will your surrender value be?

What Makes Something Valuable?

Is it because it happens to be rare?
Or is it because others stop, admire and stare?
Is it because it has a high price?
Or is it because we think it is nice?

And can how we think cause the value to soar?
By taking it away, do we value it more?
Is it because of what it can do—
Can this cause something to be precious to you?

Is it because you need it to live?
Or is it because of the gifts it will give?
Is the criteria for value outside or in?
And thinking of creational value, where to begin?

The Value of Food

There once was a wise man who had a lot of value in his life. He valued the simple things and never wanted more than he needed at the time.

One day, a lady came to visit him and help him in his work. She also offered to do his shopping for him and on her return from the stores, as she was putting the food into the fridge, she noticed how appetizing everything looked and it made her feel hungry. So she turned to the man and asked him why the food in his fridge looked so fresh, and good, and inviting, more than the food this lady had bought for herself, even though she shopped at the same store and, in fact, had some identical items in her own fridge. The man's food looked more appetizing than any food she had ever seen in her life.

"It's simple," the man replied. "We value our food more and therefore it looks tastier. We make it better by how we think about it."

Have you noticed how mama's food tastes best? Is this perhaps because of the love, value, and care she puts into it, rather than the ingredients or recipes she uses?

Telling a Secret

The whole idea of a secret is that it should be secreted away and never told. However, secrets have the way of getting out, leaking, and being told, often to just one person, who then shares it with just one other person—and so it makes its rounds in the world with everyone thinking it will stop with them. It is hard to keep a secret, because secrets want to get told, so they can grow. Have you ever heard the expression, "I am bursting to tell you…" It is the energy associated with a piece of information that is trying to be liberated from the confines of one person's mind.

The best advice about secrets, is not to repeat them. It is advisable not to say anything about another person that you would not be prepared to repeat to their face. If it is not worth saying to their face, it is probably not worth saying. A good practice, when speaking about another person who is absent is to add the codicil, "and I am prepared to say this to them." It lets the person you are talking to know that this is not a secret you are telling them.

Secrets have a way of getting back to the person they are about. Telling secrets has landed more people in trouble than any crime or misdemeanor! They have the frequency of the person they are about and, like a homing pigeon, they want to get bak to the source of their arising. Once you have told another person a secret you have been told in confidence, your subconscious has heard you say it, and it might just cause you to repeat it again.

When you tell a secret, it might be that you actually want your secret to be known, even if you ask the person you are talking to not to repeat it to anyone, and consciously you think you want the secret to be kept in confidence.

You can always ask another person not to tell you their secret, although you don't always get a chance to say that you would prefer not to hear it, because they might say it first and ask for discretion afterwards. If this happens, make the secret stop with you. Secrete it away in the vaults of your mind and try not to think about it, because if you do think about it, the energy accompanying it will be released into your aura and someone else might pick it up without you even telling them.

A secretary should be a guardian of his or her boss's secrets. However, we can all become secretaries, in the sense that we keep secrets and do not share them.

Waiting

We wait for a bus, or we wait in the doctor's waiting room, and waiting seems to be a part of life. People say to us, "Wait for me," or, "Can you wait until Monday?" Waiting is the time in which there is an anticipation of an event or occurrence that is expected to happen in the future.

However, where waiting gets dangerous is when it is associated with the idea of suspension or idleness. In other words, waiting could mean holding back one's activities, or thought processes, or the flow of one's life in anticipation of something that actually might never happen. How many times have you waited for something that didn't take place? You may have been standing on a street corner waiting for somebody who never came. Or waiting for an event that didn't happen, or waiting for a job that didn't materialize.

If you draw a line from now to an anticipated event in the future, then the space between those two points is the waiting period. What happens in our minds from the moment of anticipation to the moment of fulfillment, if such a moment indeed happens? Do we alter our state because we are waiting? Waiting successfully is an art and a skill, because if we suspend our normal going on, our activities, our ways of thinking, because something might happen in the future, then we are robbing ourselves of precious time, which could be put to productive use. Not only will we have suspended the flow of our life, but whether the anticipated event does or does not occur, it will take us time to re-engage in that flow and join the current of life.

Therefore, when we sit in a waiting room, waiting for the doctor, our life is still ticking by, and that time is just as valuable as when we might be engaged in a favorite pursuit. So there must be ways whereby we can use that time to our own advantage, to our own progression, toward our own development, so that less time gets wasted. Life is very short and, in a way, we are all waiting for that final event—death, because death can be anticipated with certainty.

If we draw a line from now to a point representing our own death, then the period between the two is waiting for death. After all, death is the only event that we can absolutely guarantee, concerning our future. However, even knowing the fact that it is something we can be certain of does not necessarily cause us to stop and suspend our ambitions and activities, cancel our aims and desires, because we know they will inevitably come to an end, together with our time on Earth. Perhaps on the contrary, because we know that final moment is coming, we might feel an urgency to fit in as much as possible between now and then.

So, why would that be different from, for example, waiting for somebody, or holding back until a person you are waiting for comes to join an activity, or a meeting? Surely the same principle can apply, in that time is always precious and we cannot have our time again.

Aging

A ten-year-old looks at a twenty-year-old and sees an adult who lives in a different world. A twenty-year-old looks at a thirty-year-old and sees someone who is definitely "past it" and "over the hill." A thirty-year-old looks at a forty-year-old and sees someone past their prime, fixed, no longer young. A forty-year-old looks at a fifty-year-old and sees someone who is slowing down and no longer up to very much. A fifty-year-old looks at a sixty-year-old and sees someone coming up to retirement, thinking of their remaining days, and losing their ambition and zest for life. A sixty-year-old looks at a seventy-year-old and wonders what it is like to be at death's door. A seventy-year-old looks at an eighty-year-old and wonders how they have managed to live so long. And yet, when we reach each of these ages ourselves, our perception changes.

Our perception of age involves comparison and relativity. As we grow older, youth stretches like an elastic, extending into our increasing years, to encompass first twenty-five, then thirty and even thirty-five. As we get older, we see that there are more younger people in the world. A sixty-year-old might even call a forty-year-old parent of grown-up children "young." Hence the saying that policemen and doctors seem to grow younger all the time. As time moves on, it seems to go faster and faster, perhaps because there is so little of it left.

Between the ages of ten and twenty, twenty and thirty,

thirty and forty, forty and fifty, fifty and sixty, sixty and seventy, seventy and eighty we are given ten years to get used to the idea that we will inevitably enter the next decade and that the next decade is also valid and, in fact, quite livable. All we need to do is find a way of thinking about entering the next decade, and being thirty, forty, or fifty, etc. There is time for values to shift; for example, during the ten years between thirty and forty the emphasis shifts from physical appearance and sexual performance to a growing concern with family, relationships, a career and/or religion. As a person grows older, their values tend to shift toward more permanent means of expression. If they do not, the person might become devastated by the deterioration of the physical body that houses the spirit, soul and electrical life.

Aging is a natural process and one of the enormous benefits of being older is that an older person knows and appreciates the feelings of a younger person, having been there themselves; a younger person can never know how someone older really feels. Within an older person there are many lives of all different ages, and experiences which with development can be called upon at will, and used to communicate with a representative of the younger generation.

If you have been to a place, you can picture it in your mind, imagine you are there and remember what it was like. If you haven't, you can only guess and imagine what it is like, but you can never really know for certain.

The 21st century western culture, in its worship of youth, has taken the dignity out of aging and the grace out of growing old. No one wants to be old any more; there is no honor in the fact of aging and the younger generations no longer cluster around to learn the wisdoms of the old, acquired on their journey of life. These times have introduced the retirement home, the old age pensioner's home, the senior citizens' apartment buildings, the retirement villages, and golfing communities. The elders of the tribe used to be the wise ones, respected and listened to by all; nowadays they are kept out of sight and in isolation, unless they are fortunate enough to continue to work, or to look after the next generation—grandparents taking care of the young children of the family. There is a natural affinity between the soon-to-depart seniors who recognize and value the brightness of the newly arrived souls.

There is a lot of insecurity and worry about getting old—older people worry about their finances, their health, and whether they will be able to care for themselves in their later years. These concerns press in on a person and are readily available, even if the person thinks they are settled to the age they are. They may be settled now to being, for example, forty, but are they prepared for and settled to being fifty, which is coming in ten years' time?

The only way to survive the business of getting older is to acquire a larger view which sees the impermanence of all things as part of Creation's plan. Our life on Earth is temporary. We were not meant to stay the same age, or live forever—we are on a journey from somewhere, and are going somewhere, too. If we view this life as but a short sojourn, and see that it is a small part of our many lives in the universe, we can be glad of and interested in every stage of the journey, for each decade brings its own revelations and learnings, and opens up new opportunities.

Living With Grace

Inherent in the human design there is an urge and a propulsion to learn, to explore, and to grow. Let's, for the sake of argument, call this the green urge, because it is similar in nature to the urge of the grass and planetary foliage, as it appears in spring and continues to grow into the summer months—it is driven by an unseen power into expansion and fulfillment. Unless a human overrides this natural urge, it will become active, and can be seen in the young child as it learns to crawl, walk, and speak. A baby knows not failure as it starts to literally find its feet, and giving up is not part of its mindset. It simply keeps on trying again and again, until it can stand up and move forward, or until it can pronounce individual words to his or her satisfaction, and begin to string those words into sentences.

This urge pushes us all the days of our life toward new learning, new understanding, new experiences, new businesses, new jobs, new hobbies, increasing wealth, new relationships, new skills, new everything. Providing the basics are taken care of, our preoccupation moves out of the realm of maintenance into the realm of "what next," which can lead to development and progression. There are those who manage to silent this urge and seem to be devoid of ambition, usually due to poor health, drug abuse, depression, lack of education, mourning, or any other reason that can pull a person away from their naturally inbuilt curiosity and need for advancement. But when it is there, this green urge is continuously causing a person to take a step away from their maintenance life into initiative, discovery, and adventure, where the unknown awaits.

When a person becomes employed in a new job, at first everything is new and interesting, as one finds one's way to the coffee machine in the morning, or learns about the phone system, or where the copier machine is located. Then there is the need to learn the names of one's co-workers, to understand the filing system, and get inside the computer programs. Once a routine has been established, and the employee begins to feel comfortable with the ways and means of the office staff, the familiar green urge will set in, unless a person enjoys the routine they have established and finds ways to advance within the job. Otherwise they might start looking around for better, more interesting employment with better pay and prospects. What was once a gratefully received position, full of promise and challenge, can become boring and routine.

So why do people often destroy or lose the very thing they say they love? Why do they not appreciate their health until they lose it, or are in danger of losing it? Why do we become familiar with what we already have? How can we safeguard against compromising what has already been achieved, to make sure that with each new adventure one does not jeopardize what has already been achieved?

The main destroyer of past achievements is familiarity. If we can safeguard against it, perhaps we will be able to value what is already part of our life, so we do not destroy or neglect our existing relationships every time something or someone new and stimulating turns up. What we already have is our platform upon which we can continue to build our future life. Do not forget the bird in hand, whether it is your home, your health, or your relationships, or simply the fact that you are able to put food on your table for one more day. An appreciation for what is already in place will provide the strength and security to venture safely into new territories, thus satisfying the green urge, as well as fostering grace as a way of life.

Permission

There are two permissions: one is what the planet will allow a human to do: we cannot fly and if we jump off a tall building, we will fall to the ground. The other permission is dictated by human law, which varies according to which country you happen to live in. Within the planetary permission there are two aspects—everything that has already been achieved on the one hand, and all that is still waiting to be discovered and implemented on the other.

What has already been accomplished are all the sports records, artistic achievements, and scientific discoveries produced so far. But every day humans pursue their dreams and new ideas and actions are added to that which already exists. We are always straddling the two permissions: that which already exists, and that which is still waiting to be achieved. It is the evolving human whose task it is to bring new discoveries from the unseen into the seen. Next year there will be new world records, new writings, new musical compositions, and new pieces of art. Technology will advance as we push back the limits of human possibility. We will improve and add to what already exists. No one knows how much more there is to learn, to know, and to accomplish, and if in fact this unchartered domain is finite or not.

As we fill out what is already possible, we increase the permission and push back the limitations to what we can be and do. When we acquire a new skill, we soon learn new depths to that ability. Take, for example, photography. A person can easily learn to hold a camera or digital phone and look for attractive landscapes, or interesting objects, to take pictures. They can point their camera and click, the picture is taken. However, soon they will realize the difference the quality of light can make to their photograph, and how it can add depth, contrast and illumination. This will open up for them a whole new level of photography, as they decide what is the best time of day to take pictures and how sunlight and moonlight add depth to objects and scenes. So now their pictures will reflect atmospheres and feelings, rather than just physical objects and scenes.

We are all born within the current band of permission, and we soon learn about the many possibilities that are open to us within that band. Within our lifetime many records will be broken, new inventions will appear, and discoveries will be made. The pioneers of each era win greater permissions, and increase the territory of what is possible. Who knows what the final record for running a mile will be? It seems that over time, just as we think we have reached the pinnacle of achievement in any field, something new appears, and records are broken…

If someone has a mission, they are more likely to add to the already existing planetary permission, bringing something new from the unseen to the seen. The moment a person decides on a particular path among many, and defines their mission in life, other pathways that go against one's chosen way and style will become eliminated and untrodden. So, for example, someone who decides to become a Catholic priest, will most probably deny themselves the experience of marriage and parenthood. Or someone who decides to become a doctor will have to dedicate a lot of their time to studies and practice, and have less time for other pursuits. It would seem that with each choice and decision one is therefore narrowing the band of permission accessible within the already limited band of permission. But at the same time one is also increasing one's ability to exercise one's faculties within that narrow band of permission, thus becoming more likely to achieve something no one else has ever been able to achieve. If someone becomes a doctor and specializes as, say, an eye surgeon, one will become more likely to find a new cure for an eye disease.

Within the domain of a person's mission they are more liable to push back the barriers of human limitation to enlarge the availability of new permissions.

Perhaps permission is granted to the human race from the universe, and on its evolutionary journey through time there have been specific moments when new permissions have been granted. Perhaps we need to fill out the permissions already given before new permissions are attracted by those humans who are innovative within their chosen field, so that human development can become a reality.

Assumption

Assumption closes a person off from the reality of their situation. They assume they know what will happen, or how another person feels, when they haven't got the correct information, or haven't bothered to find out. It is a mental short cut, and it says, "I know already." It is a premature leap to conclusions, and an attempt to fit one's understanding of one's situation into pre-established categories and definitions. Life never repeats itself, and nothing ever turns out exactly as we expect it; we can never know all the parameters and influences at play—there are simply too many, and everything is changing all the time.

How many times have you planned to do something, given yourself plenty of time, but still ended up rushing, and almost being late for an appointment or meeting, simply because of unexpected circumstances? Who factors in a puncture, or the fact that the phone might run out of juice? And what about an unexpected emergency that you have to attend to? Maybe a child is ill, or a friend has an accident. Things do happen, as we well know. So why assume anything will go exactly the way we want it to?

Even when things seem to be going according to plan, there is always the chance that that could change, or that the sequence of events will spark off new events in the future, currently beyond our comprehension and scope. If by thinking something you can make it happen, perhaps by assuming how the situation will turn out, we are blocking future events, causing stagnation and preventing change. If you expect another to be "the same old predictable self," maybe you are contributing to their lack of development. But if you give them the benefit of the doubt, and don't assume you know what they will do, maybe you will encourage them to grow. Maybe they will surprise you with what they know and what they can do.

There is a saying about the impossibility of being a prophet in one's own country. Perhaps we need to travel outside the surrounding ring of assumption to break into new territories, and discover our higher selves. Assumption, like all energetic properties, begins with oneself. When you wake up in the morning, maybe you are born anew, and there is some new energy coursing through you. It never is "just another day."

Every person is different and has their own unique needs, timings, and requirements. To expect another to comply with our own expectancies, standards and demands is to miss the opportunity to learn from another person's way and style, and to understand their reasons for doing what they do. Assumption causes a person to measure the character and life of another through the keyhole of one's own limited history and experience.

To assume that anything remains the same is to deny oneself the adventure of change and new beginnings. Even when going to bed at night, we assume we will get up in the morning, and that everything will be as we had left it, thus blinding ourselves to change, and ignoring the newness of each passing day. Just look at a photograph of yourself from ten, or twenty years ago, and note how you have changed. It did not happen all at once, but little by little, with each passing day.

We leave assumption behind when we visit new places, encounter new situations, or meet new people. Our faculties become alert, observant, interested and challenged, and we are ready to take in new information. But even then, we tend to compare what we are encountering with what we already know, and are familiar with, rather than absorbing the newness of the situation, and giving it an independent lease of life within our memory banks.

Assumption weakens value and halts development. When external circumstances change, we get pulled out of assumption and our value for life increases.

There is an old Persian story of a carpet seller and a woman who was looking for a bargain. He stated his price for his carpets and gave her a limited time to make up her mind. As the time elapsed and she had not agreed to his price, he proceeded to throw, one by one, the precious carpets onto the fire. In the end, the woman could take it no longer and ended up paying the price for the last carpet that she could have paid for the lot, if she had made her mind up earlier. If you value something, be prepared to pay the price for having it.

Our faculty becomes less astute when we assume the situation or person we are dealing with is the same as we had encountered before. However, everything and everybody is changing all the time. No two days, weeks or months are the same. Nothing in our life is guaranteed—everything is increasing or decreasing all the time. As you are reading these words, you are changing, too, and are subject to the cosmic energetic cycles that wash over us every single day. As planet Earth hurtles through space and revolves on its axis, it enters forever new spaces within the universal expanses, bringing new experiences, essences, and forever opening up new possibilities. To be joined to the universe is to be open and full of wonder, never knowing what will happen next.

Assumption can deny a person the opportunity of progress. Today you are older and wiser, with more experience and wisdom, than you were yesterday. You are closer to death than you ever have been. You have fewer days left than yesterday. Value your time now and fill your days with meaning and value, so that you can make a return for the gift of life. Do not allow assumption to fix you and your life according to what has already been, thus limiting you potential and power of discovery.

Give and Take

Give and take describes a bilateral exchange between people where there is tolerance, understanding, and a willingness to compromise when disagreements arise. In order to establish a harmonious relationship, one needs to consider the wants and needs of the other person and not insist on one's own requirements and preferences as a priority; at least not all the time. The expression "give and take" is used to explain why one cannot always have one's way and that other people might have interests that conflict with our own.

Some people grow up to be givers; others become takers. Most of us are a mix of both—sometimes we give, and sometimes we take. We are usually more willing givers with our family and loved ones; if we share our life with someone, we learn when to give and when to take.

The planet gives us our food and our air to breathe; she provides us with the nutrients we need, and we are used to taking from her our daily supply of four foods: physical food, liquids, air and energy. There is a law that says that the full runs to the empty. So in any exchange between people it will be the weaker who takes from the stronger. A person who is energetically strong would normally become a giver in a mutual relationship with a weaker person. However, generosity is a human quality, but so is greed. So sometimes a strong person will take from the weaker because he or she is not sensitive to the needs of another.

When we were born, we were given everything we needed to live, and this generosity of the planet and our parents, or caregivers, has continued to this day. We can also connect to higher energies that are transmitted from the universe and partake of this table of plenty that is afforded to us. The word partake is more fitting here, because it suggests conscious participation, rather than the word take, which suggests a one-sided action. When connected to higher energies, a person can give to another and not become depleted themselves, because there will always be further supplies available. This is what is meant by the biblical expression, "My cup runneth over." A person with universal development will be connected to higher energies, and will always be the giver in any relationship, because there is no one for them to take from. They will be glad to give, however, because giving will be for them a way of life. Instead of give and take, they will give to receive.

One way to become a giver, rather than a taker, is to ask oneself the question, "What can I give in this situation?" rather than, "What can I get in this situation?" This question can be asked at any moment of one's life. As we are processors of energy, we are always giving and receiving. Every thought is a transmission and it connects us to people and places, from which we can then draw energy in return. What part do we want to play within this feast that planetary life offers us? We take part in creation, but we also give parts back.

At birth we received our body, our mind, our soul, our five senses, and all the talents and inclinations which we later developed. These gifts create a platform upon which further gifts can be received. We have everything we need to create a productive, rewarding and universally connected life. Our gifts and our talents are meant to be shared, to inspire others, and create moments of rich exchange.

If we expect to earn what we get, we will be happy to work for our rewards, and to not insist on instant gratification, because the universe has its own timings and works in mysterious ways. Our projection of what we might receive is limited to what we already know, whereas the planet is continuously receiving new and original universal energies. Energy cannot be destroyed and "what goes round, comes around." If you decide to be giving as a way of life, you will also receive. Energy that is not circulating becomes stale, so you cannot accumulate force or electrical wealth, like putting money in the bank, but by giving it away, you will earn more.

Rather than a taker, a giver be
And a richer life you will surely see.

Security

For most people home represents security; good or bad, it is what they know, what they have experienced, the area within which they feel comfortable, familiar, well-established. If things go wrong, they run for home—the known territory where the rules are understood and assimilated, where every corner and path is recognized, where habits and customs are practiced, where well-trodden areas are made safe; where there are no surprises, no sudden changes, no unexpected demands. Unlike being at home, exploration into new territories might seem risky and unpredictable.

Fear of the unknown is what prevents most people from exploring new territories. It causes a person to back off from a new situation into familiar surroundings that are like a well worn garment that fits around our every move or weakness. If our past experiences were to be represented by a box, then the limitless possibility of what we could become lies outside that box. Anything new, any new situation, every undiscovered piece of ground, all un-thought thoughts, unheard sounds, unseen sights, unsmelt scents, untouched objects—they all represent our possible future, as long as we are prepared to come out of the box into what is new. We are like a small dot inside a huge expanse of space. If we take, as an example, all the places we have visited in our life and compare them to all the places on Earth to which we have not yet been, it is hard to imagine a graphic way to represent such a comparison—the difference between the two would be so large.

How many homes have we lived in? How many more have we visited? How many homes are there on planet Earth? If we have visited fifty homes, and on average there are five people per home, then we are missing over a million three hundred thousand homes that we have never set foot in. That figure represents the present, but there are many more homes that existed in the past and will be built in the future, and are being built at this very moment ,that we have not seen and will not visit.

Perhaps we can change our thinking and decide that the box representing our experience has brought us to this moment in the present, but the future and our development lie outside that box. New learning, new knowledge, and new experience gained from outside the box will allow us to expand our box and add to our energetic profile, which lives inside our aura, or energy field.

Human evolution depends on innovation, inspiration, creativity and change, all of which lie outside the box that contains our history. So feeling secure that this planet has a future also lies outside the box. We are summoned to the great expanse of what is new in the universe at this moment, and to the novelty of the next one.

Change

There is a saying that change is the only constant in our lives. And yet, we seek stability and constancy, while at the same time trying to improve our lot, and being constantly interested in what is new. Our lives are a continuous adjustment to reconcile change with habits, and established patterns of behavior.

We are used to observing nature's cycles, and expect summer to follow spring, and fall to appear after summer. We rely on this regularity to the point that our livelihood depends on it. However, no two summers are the same, and every fall brings with it a new sequence of events, which causes a new palette of color, and a unique display of light, shade, and hue. The weather is a topic of endless conversations and is probably the most talked about subject on planet Earth.

If we had a longer view, and could see the seasons in term of thousands, or even millions of years, rather than the few decades we might have experienced within our lifetime, we would probably be astonished at the multiple changes in our world—we would witness ice ages, continental shifts, and multiple polarity changes; we would see earthquakes and volcanic eruptions that have changed the cartographic profile of the planet we live in. Alongside planetary developments, we would also witness the coming and going of species and the evolution of the human kind.

Even in our lifetime, the political map has changed several times already and these days regular replacements of maps must be planned for in school budgets. So we should not be surprised that our own makeup shifts with the sands of time, and that imperceptibly, day by day, we are changing and altering to the point where major displacements might be needed to abruptly adjust to our new circumstance. This could be a physical requirement, like a need for an operation, or a change in the family circumstance, like a divorce, or a child leaving home to start a life on their own. Such a change might seem sudden at the time, but it probably had a long history arriving. A change can be seen as an improvement or as a worsening condition. A debilitating disease can be the result of unfortunate lifestyle choices over a long period of time, and sometimes, looking back, we can see that the warning signs were there, and that we should have "known better" earlier. We tend to ignore what we do not want to know.

A regenerative change has its history too, and if a person works at something day by day, they will see results of their efforts, which will gradually bring change to their life. They might become an expert at something, or an authority in their field. Perfection does not leave room for improvement, so in a changing world, perhaps the adage should be, "Practice makes better."

As I write these words, there are over seven billion people in the world, and they are all changing all the time. Tomorrow there will be seven billion slightly altered people. The question we might want ask is, "Are we getting better, or are we getting worse as we age?"

Blame and Excuses

Blame and excuses are both aspects of the same syndrome —they are an attempt to divert responsibility for an action (or lack of action) from oneself. Blame is a directed excuse, usually involving another person or group. Excuses are usually directed at external circumstances.

Blame

Blame is an escape from responsibility, and is caused by a person being unwilling to face reality and the results of one's own actions. It temporarily relieves the pressure, but as a result, it distorts reality and bends the facts to support its claim. Blame is usually created by someone who has difficulty handling pressure. If a person blames someone else for something they are responsible for, it might relieve pressure at first, but it will cause a dichotomy between the conscious and unconscious brain.

By blaming someone else for one's actions, a person is creating a story that is biased, and false. A person can even convince oneself that their story is true, and end up remembering only those details which support one's claim. We remember what we want to remember and what supports our beliefs and theories concerning other people.

To avoid blaming others for one's mistakes, it is important to be dedicated to the truth, and to try to understand the reality of any given situation. There are usually two sides to every story, and understanding another person's viewpoint is essential in developing a "third vector view." Being impartial will save a person from blame and lead one to understanding the motivations behind another person's action. Why a person did something then becomes more important than the fact that they did it. Just as we are, another person is also subject to the energies, forces, passions, and feelings that move through them, according to their character formation and previous experience. We express the unseen worlds by being motivated by such essences as care, or hope, or jealousy, or ambition. When an essence moves through a person, like, for example, the essence of care, they will become known as a caring person. The original essence of care exists within the energy fields of planet Earth and contains all the care that has ever been experienced by humans throughout history. Essences are alive and they manifest through people— that is how they become invigorated, re-animated and awakened from their dormant state; this is how they grow.

A third vector view allows a person to appreciate the energies appearing through another human, rather than criticizing (or lauding) the person. A child should be told, "That was an inconsiderate thing to do," but never "You are a bad boy." So the third vector is never personal, but will facilitate understanding, and will help offer reflections to another that will be fair and impartial.

Only the humans are subject to blame; an oak tree will not blame a pine tree for growing a little too close for comfort, and blocking out the sun. If a person knows who they are, knows what they are like, and knows what they want, they will not blame others for the predicament they find themselves in. One often hears sentences beginning with "They…" in which a person might accuse these mysterious "theys" of being irresponsible, guilty or stupid.

Who does not blame others for their past mistakes? Who has not had relationships, business dealings, or family affairs that were messed up and ended badly? Who has not had teachers who were unfair, and unnecessarily critical of their abilities and work? But when we understand that others are doing the best they can, and they might be acting out of ignorance, or through misunderstanding, blame seems to melt away. Who would we be if we did not sometimes have what now seem like unfortunate encounters with others? Perhaps we have learned valuable lessons at the hands of others, and we are now much wiser because we have been educated by their mistakes. When we disapprove of others, when they do not live up to our expectations, or when we think we know better, we are questioning our own standards, and thinking of ways the actions of others could be improved. We can always write the criticism of others in a positive light—as an attempt to find better ways and means. We can also rewrite our past, when we realize how other people are not perfect, and how our teachers, mentors and parents were trying to do their best.

Then we must also realize that others might be blaming us for our mistakes, and our past actions. It is important to not carry forward guilt and shame, which are related to blame, but are directed toward oneself. Both these essences have a dampening effect, and can cause a person to become weak when they are required to pioneer a new project, to start a new relationship, or begin a new career path.

When you find a flaw in the behavior of another, or

spot a mistake, or see clearly how they could have done something better, or more effectively, do you make fun, criticize and judge, or do you pass on your suggestions without a feeling of superiority and satisfaction? If blame is going to retreat from your aura, you need to face your own mistakes, which are probably not so bad, and accept that others will have different ways of doing things.

Excuses

Excuses are not necessarily pointed at another person or event, but like blame, they are also an attempt to shift responsibility away from oneself. Some excuses become proverbial, like "The dog ate my homework," or the illness of a grandmother or other distant relative prevented one from completing a task. "The finger and the head are school excuses," the old Polish rhyming proverb says.

The antidote to both blame and excuses is to decide to take full responsibility for one's actions, as well as one's non-actions. This is an important step in taking control of one's life. Blame energetically connects one to the person one blames, or to the circumstance which one sees to be the cause of one's actions; deciding not to blame anyone or anything releases one from this dependence and will give you more energy. Confirmation and acceptance come from the inside first. If you value yourself, others will learn to appreciate who you are, too. If a person is settled with their choices and their decisions, there will be no need for blame or excuses. Even though sometimes things do not turn out as we have planned, and unexpected obstacles will always find their way into our lives, if our actions are deliberate and purposeful, then unforeseen results will be welcomed. It is these unexpected events that are responsible for the majority of discoveries, inventions, and new ideas. They can be seen as challenges to be overcome, or as a learning how not to proceed in the future.

Love the truth as a first principle, because the truth is what is and is not tainted by personal bias. The saying "God is with us," used throughout history by warring factions demonstrates that those fighters who made this claim had departed from the path of truth. How can God support one side against another? Or how can God support both sides against each other? If you live, God is with you. The question is, are you with God?

Gain and Loss

The journey through life is a continuum of gain and loss, ups and downs, wins and losses. We assess each day and looking back there are "good days" and "bad days," as well as "ongoing life days," which are neither good nor bad. It depends on what happens each day, who we meet, where we go, what we do, how we feel, and whether at the end of the day there is a sense of having learned something, gained something, spent time usefully and enjoyably, or whether we had lost something, forgot something, wasted time, couldn't get to what we had intended to get to, and therefore felt regret or loss.

What happens if, instead of looking at each day at a time, you look at a week, a month, a year, or even a decade (depending on how old you are)? It is like the stock market—it goes up and down on a daily basis—a little here, a little bit more there—but you only get a realistic view of whether the prevailing trend is a bear market or a bull market when you look at a longer span of time. It is the same with our ongoing life: we have a certain view of how things are going, and how we might wish they would progress. But to get a true view of one's progress, it is important to stop sometimes and take a deeper look by comparing today and now to, say, the same time last year, or five years ago. Are things really as bad (or as good) as they seem?

Prejudice Versus Respect

The root of the word prejudice means to pre-judge—to form an opinion about something without checking whether it is based in fact.

If we wait until we can check the facts, and weigh the evidence, we can then form a judgment or an assessment.

If, however, we then look again, we are showing our respect, because that is what the root of the word respect means —to look again (from *spectare*—to look in Latin).

So, the longer we take to check the facts and to re-examine whether our opinions are true or not, the further away from prejudice we travel toward the quality of respect.

Note:
This does not mean that if we take time to investigate a negative action or quality, like murder or jealousy, we come to respect it. It simply means that we are demonstrating respect for the process itself and thereby for our own stance in relation to it.

High and Low Energies

Just as there are places in the world where high energies gather, so there are places where lower energies congregate. They live in these locations due to crimes committed in the past, due to wars fought, or battles waged—all because of human activity originating from the lower levels of energies within the astral light.

You could refer to them as energy worlds scars—haunted houses, for example, where people see ghosts or hear noises and moans that cannot be attributed to the living. There are castles and palaces, battlefields and church cemeteries where the dead speak to those who are sensitive, and able to understand their language, or see images that others cannot.

At St. Mark's Church In-The-Bowery in New York City, for example, many people have heard a repetitive thump which is believed to be the sound of Peter Stuyvesant's wooden leg as he roams the church many years after his death. Peter Stuyvesant, the last director-general of the colony of New Netherland, which later became New York, was buried in a crypt underneath the church in 1672. He had lost his leg in 1644 when he led an attack on the Island of Saint Martin, which was then held by the Spanish.

In Chichen Itza in Mexico, at the site of the ancient pyramid, observatory, temples and other constructions, there are both high and low energies which can be detected and felt. It was originally a place of meditation, learning and spiritual ceremonies, where the ancient Mayans could observe the movement of the planets and the stars in the ancient observatory. However, later it became the site of human sacrifice, after the Aztecs and the Toltecs took over the site. If you have the opportunity to visit this place, your guide might ask you how you are caused to feel in particular parts of the site, and whether some areas make you feel happy and relaxed, while others make you feel sad.

When visiting X'ian in China, I was invited to go to the mausoleum created by Emperor Qin Shi Huang, the same ruler who had created the famous terra-cotta army which has been seen in exhibits by millions of people all over the world as it travelled throughout Europe and North America. What is perhaps not so well known is that the terra-cotta army was designed to accompany the emperor on his journey to heaven where he hoped to conquer and consequently rule in the celestial mansion. Once the construction of the terra-cotta army was finished, those who designed and sculpted it were killed and the army remained buried until it was discovered in a field in 1974.

The terra-cotta soldiers are known by many, but what is not so well known is that Emperor Qin Shi Huang also built a mausoleum to himself at another location where he buried hundreds of clay and wooden figures as well as many clay representations of cows, sheep, pigs, dogs, and other animals, so that they could accompany him into the next world. When I visited this site there were very few people there, the lights were kept low, and the atmosphere of the place had an eerie feel to it. After being there for a while—the site is large with several pits full of figures that one can observe from above, walking along glass sheets covering the trenches—I suddenly felt a pain in my jaws and then a pressure on my chest. I thought I was having a heart attack and that I was surely going to die. Breathing became shallow and difficult and I had to get out of there. I prayed not to die in a foreign location and to be allowed to get home to die in my own bed. As I emerged from the mausoleum into the sunlight I was still struggling to catch my breath. I asked the driver who had brought me there to take me to the airport. I do not know whether he felt anything, but he seemed in a hurry to leave me beside the terminal entrance, throwing my coat on the ground and quickly driving away.

I somehow managed to check in and get through security, after which I bought a cup of tea, sat down and continued to pray. I then remembered that the guide had told me that when Emperor Qin Shi Huang died, he had many of his concubines buried alive with him. If they were gagged and then earth thrown onto their bodies, they likely would have felt a pain similar to the pain I had just experienced. I believe I had connected to an energetic trace of the women's pain which still remains on the site of their last resting place.

As I realized what was happening to me, I felt a surge of energy that was healing and reassuring in its nature. The pain was lifted from me and I felt a great sense of wellbeing, as if I was being healed, supported and embraced by a universal entity. I thanked the healing "angel" and was soon on my way home.

Being Clean

"Clean people do not need to wash." This is a phrase we used as children when we wanted to escape the obligatory duty of having to wash before going to bed, in order to extend our play time a little bit more. However, it never worked.

But if you are clean, why would you need to wash? Of course, after a day of play, a child will not be clean. We stay clean by regularly washing, bathing and showering, taking advantage of the cleansing properties of water and soap. So clean people repetitively wash, but they do get dirty, just like everyone else who lives on planet Earth and is subject to the influence of dust and various pollutants to be found in the air, and upon the ground.

It is easy to see how we keep ourselves physically clean, but what about clean energy? If we decide to be patient, for example, it is not enough to be patient once, twice, or a few times. It is necessary to keep that essence alive in our aura, so it can influence our behavior and responses. Just as the heart needs to be exercised at least a couple of times a week to maintain fitness, so do our qualities that we have decided to bring into our lives. First we decide we want to be a certain way—say, courageous or honest; then we invite those essences into our life by behaving according to those qualities. Then there comes a time when these qualities take up permanent residence within our energy field and we automatically and instantaneously respond in any situation in a way that embodies those qualities.

A young ingenue might look at an older, experienced actress and envy her her skill and fame. But the older actress was once a young ingenue and had honed her skills over years of rehearsals, performances, and hard word. People might envy you what you have or who you are, but you know the time it has taken for you to become who you are, and to do what you can do. You have worked to develop your skills, and now they are part of you and represent who you are.

Apart from the automatic development through childhood, puberty, into adolescence and adulthood, everything we are has been acquired by repetition and hard work. If we had done something only once or twice, we cannot claim it as part of our skill set or character formation. Where is the famous piano player who has touched the keyboard only once, or the proficient typist who has only typed one letter using one finger? A young mother is indeed a mother the day her child is born, but it will take days and months of caring for her child for her to become experienced and confident in her parenting skills. The term mother does not imply skill or training, or quality, but being clean does.

Colors in the Aura

New Age shows, like New World Expo in New York and Florida, or the Total Health Show held every year in Toronto, Canada usually include a booth offering to take photographs of a person's aura with the help of Kirilian photography. This technique utilizes voltage which enables subtle energies to make a mark on a photographic plate.

The photograph resulting from this process shows the colors in a person's aura at the moment the photograph was taken, when the subject had braced himself or herself for the photo, hand on an electrified plate, in anticipation of their big energy moment.

Such a photograph does indeed show the colors in the aura at that moment when the photograph is taken. But a moment later, as the person relaxes, the colors will most probably change, because colors in the aura are in constant transition as our thoughts, feelings, and behaviors change from moment to moment.

Having had their aura photograph taken at a show, people might proudly declare, "My aura is purple," or "red," or "blue," or any color that appears in the photograph. But even as they say it, it is probably no longer true, as their thoughts turn to other matters and, once again, the subtle colors change.

Seeing and reading colors in the aura is helpful in trying to determine what is going on in a person's life at any given moment. Someone who is exercising, or involved in military activity, might have red in their aura, which also denotes such qualities as determination, or administrative abilities.

Blue can indicate a peaceful mood, and yellow might mean that a person is feeling emotional about something. Of course, every color could mean many things, depending on hue and shade. Green, for example, could be a sign of creativity, or of a healing energy presence in the aura.

But whatever the color, it is the shade and illumination that indicate the level of energy present within a person's aura at any given moment. And whatever the color, it will probably change within minutes as our thoughts turn to new issues and our feelings register new sentiments.

Every Moment Counts

Everyone agrees that the older you get, the faster time seems to fly. The seasons and the years do not linger long, and before you know it, another birthday has added another unit to your age.

Isn't it strange how we guess the age of everyone we meet, describing people as "middle-aged," "old" or "young"? A person's age is the most impermanent attribute you could possibly use to describe them. As we get older, professional people we deal with, like doctors, policemen and salespeople seem to get younger and younger. As time flies by, there is less and less of it left, and it becomes more and more precious. If we knew the time and date of our departure, also known as death, would we alter our behavior, knowing exactly how much more time we had left? We know our birthday and celebrate it every year. But if we consider that our death could be a birth into something new, perhaps it would be a far greater reason to celebrate than our birthday.

Perhaps time is speeding up, because even young people are noticing the accelerated passage of time. We used to think we had all the time in the world, that we were immortal, and that aging was something that happened to everyone else. Perhaps there is a new urgency abroad, a knowing that these moments we still have are flecting, and will never be ours again to squander or savor, depending on our inclination and choice.

If you know what you want in this life, perhaps there is still time to achieve it. If you don't, then how can anything or anyone help you? If you don't, how can you make decisions about how you are going to spend your time, the most precious commodity you have? Never mind gold and silver, riches and jewels; time will allow you to achieve everything you want, and more. Without it, we have come to the end of our journey and there is no more for us to do, or be, or achieve.

Spend your time wisely. Learn now not to suffer fools gladly, or waste time, to speak your mind, and go for what you want, thus living the wisdom of old age today. Most people learn these things when it is already too late. How much time do you have left? No one knows, not even you. Whatever the answer, it is not much, and you have probably used up at least a quarter of it already. Look back at your past to see how you have spent your time thus far, and from that viewpoint, make a decision whether you want your future to be different. If so, start now, and introduce the changes you want to see in your life; begin to take control of your life, for your time is now, and this is the time of your life.

As the sands of your time sift through the hourglass of your life, you are positioned in the present moment between the past and the future, where you can decide and manage who you want to become. Can you afford to waste one grain of time, and lose your sense of value and appreciation for every single moment that is still left?

Linking and Thinking

Mostly people do not think; they link. Linking is associating images, events, memories. A woman might look in a shop window, for example, and see a green dress which reminds her of a dress she had when she was 18. Her mind then drifts back to her college days and her first boyfriend. She then wonders what has happened to him and she remembers that she had seen his picture in the paper a while back. Was it because he was a lawyer, and the article was about a case he was defending? she wonders. And so the links continue. She might then carry on walking down the street, and as she passes a drugstore, she remembers that she has run out of washing up liquid, and that she has to buy some. She looks at her watch and notices it is late, so she decides to pop in to the store on her way home. And so it continues.

This is not thinking, but linking. Thanking is deliberately, consciously picking a subject and creatively thinking it through—looking at all the arguments, exhausting the subject, and bringing the matter to a conclusion, whether it is final or an interim staging post. Real thinking has a continuous nature and is cooling to the systems—it is very good for the brain; it is a bit like taking your brain to the gym. The more you exercise, the easier it becomes. In our fragmented and busy world, we mostly have little time for real thinking, but to do so regularly will pay back in abundance. It allows a person to become quiet inside and to follow a train of thought; it might be surprising and inspiring to see where it leads.

So take a little time each day to think about your life, and matters that are important to you. It will bring clarity of understanding, and an enhanced perspective on your future and your goals. It will help you achieve your dreams, and will improve your relationships.

Points of View

Everyone has a unique point of view. Each of our points of view is different from other people's because we can only see a small part of the picture at any particular time. The old story about the elephant says it well—six people are looking at the same animal, but each sees something different, because they are only seeing a partial view. The one looking at the leg will say he sees a grey column covered in wrinkled, leathery material; the one looking at the tail will say he sees a rope hanging down and, maybe it is used to ring a bell; a third looking at the trunk will say he is looking up a tube; a fourth person looking at the ear will say they see large floppy material that could be a kite.

When different people go into the forest, they see different things, and have different experiences. How they view the forest will depend on many things: their experience, their desires, their goals, their ways of thinking, their interests, and their passions. So, for example, a paper manufacturer will go into the woods and be able to assess how much paper he could make from the trees he sees. A property developer might think about building a resort in the forest, assessing where to construct his hotel, where to build a road, which trees to save, and how much money he could make. An environmentalist would wish there were more forests on Earth, and might plan to plant more trees. A meditator might look for a good place to meditate. An artist will look for a picturesque spot to paint the view, and a photographer will look for a place where color and light play together, creating an ideal image to be photographed. Each of these people will have a completely different experience, and will describe their walk in the woods in a unique way. Wherever we go, it is like walking in the woods—we take our experiences and desires with us, and we look at the world around us through the lens of our personality.

Here are seven ways of viewing the world. (They are hypothetical because no one is just one thing—we are combinations and conglomerates of thoughts, feelings and levels of energy.)

At the lowest level of energy a person is preoccupied with self, and not really interested in the feelings, or needs of other people. This is the level of the narcissist and selfish person, and the egoist whose main desire is to please himself. It is difficult to be friends with such a person, or to enter into an intimate relationship with them, because in every situation they will be promoting themselves, and not care about the feelings of the other person. If you tell them a story about what had happened to you, they will immediately tell you a story about their own exploits; if you tell them about your wishes and desires, they will discount them and tell you about their own, expecting you to help them fulfill them.

The next level contains people who are preoccupied with family; they are selfless in their devotion to their loved ones, but this is where their altruism ends. Their concerns do not extend beyond the walls of the home. People at this level are preoccupied with maintenance and the day to day struggle to make ends meet. A good example of such a person is a mother who has several children and spends her days caring for them, earning money to pay for their education and keep, and does not have time to further her own education or widen her circle of interests and friends. Of course, in time, as the children grow up, she might become interested in learning a new skill, and developing new habits. We are never just processing one level of energy; we can develop and improve with age, or deteriorate as we adopt harmful habits, and process lower energies.

The person at the fifth level has a concern for their community—their point of view extends beyond their immediate family to their friends and neighbors. This could be someone who is active locally, trying to improve the neighborhood, perhaps volunteering at a soup kitchen, or being a member of the Parents Teachers Association. They might be on a local committee, planning ways to improve the district, and helping others, specially those less fortunate than themselves.

People at the next level want to improve the whole area or town; they might be a candidate for the mayor. They have a vision for the future and usually end up in the town hall, making decisions on behalf of everyone else in the district.

The next level represents people who have a national view and are concerned for the fate of the whole country they live in. These are people who are prone to go into politics, and to advocate for change. They have big ideas about what needs to be done, and they will gladly donate their time to help elect the people they feel are fit to govern.

People at the next level have a global view and are interested in the future of our world. They might be environmentalists, or world travelers, or activists in a non-governmental organization. They will fight poverty, hunger, or pollution, and be an ambassador for goodwill. They are interested in politics, history and social sciences, and they will be concerned about global issues, including, for example, the United Nations Millennium Goals. They will understand issues on a global scale and their concerns might take them to the four corners of the world where they will see the plight of other peoples and nations first hand.

The person with the largest view of all is someone who has a universal view. This is a person who thinks about their next life after this one, whether they believe in reincarnation, or some form of life after death. They believe they are here on Earth for a purpose, and are concerned about their legacy. It could be an astronomer who observes the movements of the planets and the stars, and tracks the connections between the positions of planets in the skies, and the fates of human beings, or an astronaut who has traveled beyond the Earth, and has observed our planet from outer space. People at this level believe we are not alone, and that there are entities and intelligent beings on other planets and stars. Like the Egyptians, they see that life is not limited to our years on this planet, but that life extends into the millions of years. We have come from somewhere and are going somewhere, and perhaps a person at this level would consider where they would want to be born into their next life after they die, because perhaps there are many options available, and if we decide where we want to reincarnate, we will have a better chance of going there.

Most people have many points of view, and are not restricted to any one level. Sometimes we might be self absorbed, whereas at other times we might become concerned about our neighborhood, or carefully consider who we want to vote for in an election, so the country we live in can have the best chance of becoming prosperous and rich. Throughout a lifetime our interests, concerns, and preoccupations change; a teenager is more concerned about self; a young parent will be absorbed by the demands of parenthood, and have a deepened concern for the wellbeing of their family; in later years a person might become more preoccupied with national, global, and universal issues. As we approach the end of life we might become more interested in religion, and the possibility of life after death. We can chart our development according to these levels, and observe how other people, as well as ourselves, move from one level of interest to another.

Talking About Others

It is important to understand that thoughts, words, and conversations are accompanied by energy. If we think of another place or person, the energy of that thought seeks its destination out and goes to it, because it is on the same frequency. When you suddenly and unexpectedly think of another person, it might be that they were thinking of you at the same time. Have you ever picked up your phone to connect to someone, only to find that they were phoning you at the same time? If you think of someone in anger, that anger will go to the other person, too. If you think with compassion, compassion will travel to its destination. So will love, support, encouragement, or any of a myriad of other essences, both positive and negative. That is why it is important to be careful what you think, because love and compassion will enhance a person (even though they might not know why they are suddenly feeling uplifted and inspired); anger and blame will depress them and make them feel worse. So when thinking of another person, even if they had done something that according to you was wrong, try to send them encouragement to be a better person, and get rid of the resentment or disappointment you might feel toward them.

How do you feel when others speak about you? If they praise you and appreciate you for who you are, you feel pleased and satisfied; if they criticize you, you might feel upset and hurt. We all want to be wanted, and loved, and valued. To receive the energies of such essences as love, we need to send them out first, so that a little bit of these high energies becomes part of our energetic make-up. "To get gold, you need to first have a little gold," the saying goes. Think well of your friends and other people, and that essence of appreciation will come back to you. What you give out will come back to you. "What goes round comes around."

If you talk about another person, they will know it, though perhaps not consciously. If they are sensitive, they will pick up looks and behavior patterns that will tell them they have been the subject of a conversation among acquaintances or friends.

The only reason to talk about someone behind their back is to help, educate or explain. Before launching into a conversation about another person, it is useful to call over your value for that person. It will allow you to come from an impartial place, and become energetically clear how you feel about another person. It will also add to the value for that person that already exists in the energy worlds of the planet. Another consideration is the fact that whatever you say and how you feel about that person when saying it will return to the source of its arising, which is that person's energy field. Positive thoughts strengthen a person, while negative ones weaken them.

Asking for Help

Energies come from all levels, so when petitioning to connect to the energy worlds, it is important to specify which level of energy one wishes to connect to. Because both energies—high and low—may respond to a petition for guidance or a cry for help.

I believe there are energies and forces that do come when we ask for help; maybe our guardian angels look after us in our hour of need, or maybe deceased parents, or other family members remain close to us after their departure from the physical plane. Whatever name we give to these energy helpers, there are stories from around the world that confirm that miraculous healing and reversals of fate can, and do occur.

Some years ago my husband David and I lived in Canada, an hour and a half's drive north from the city of Toronto, in a little place called Lisle. We would often drive into the city for work. Sometimes in the winter in Ontario there can be a brief thaw, and then it might rain and the rain freezes over, creating hazardous driving conditions on the road. On one such winter morning I was driving into the city, noticing on the side of the road several vehicles which had skidded into the ditch or had bumped into each other. The police were busy that morning, as I passed several police cars engaged with drivers. I was driving carefully, aware of the difficult road conditions. Then, unexpectedly, I hit a sheet of ice and the car was dramatically turned sideways; it was now fast hurtling toward the metal barrier in the middle of the dual lane highway. I knew I was heading toward a crash and wondered whether the car would be totalled and whether I would escape from this pending accident alive. The car must have been sliding across the road at at least forty miles an hour. I knew that braking would make it worse, so I just watched as the barrier was rushing toward me.

I cried out for help, firmly believing that there might be an angel or some rescuing presence that could save my life. Never mind the car, I realized it was too late to save it from the impact. "Help," I cried out loud. And then a miraculous thing happened—something I cannot explain to this day. From rushing headlong into a disaster, the car suddenly stopped, an inch away from the barrier, as if some unseen hand had halted it in its tracks. I could not believe it. I sat there for a moment, dazed and blinking incredulously, shaking from the adrenaline rush and thanking my unseen protector. And then, as if to warn me, and as if the car was being pushed from behind, it gently banged into the barrier and stopped again. I was able to back away from the barrier and continue my drive into the city.

When I arrived at my destination and checked the car from bumper to bumper, but there was not even a scratch on it. To this day I consider that experience to be a miraculous demonstration of the power of the energy worlds.

I often do ask the unseen energies that support our lives for help, and I do believe that help is often manifested in mysterious and sometimes not-so-obvious ways. Asking for help can not only bring resolution to problems, or answers to questions, but, more importantly, it demonstrates that we believe in the power of the unseen worlds, and in the fact that in this life we are not alone and simply never will be.

Sacred Sites

When you visit an ancient site, or a religious building, like a church, a mosque, or a synagogue, you might often wonder about the energy of the place, and why it does not feel holy or sacred. There are places in the world that are energy vortices where ancient civilizations built their monuments to honor the energy of the place, and to conduct their celebrations within the aura of higher energy vibrations. Often these ancient sites become attractive tourist destinations with a multitude of people wandering through, taking pictures, and then moving on to the next attraction on their busy itinerary.

Natural energies are sensitive to human activities and human intentions, and tend to shy away from throngs of people whose main motivation is curiosity, and the quest for the perfect photograph. So where do these higher energies that inspired ancient civilizations to build their monuments and places of worship hide? They often can be found in places where few people go, and where it is possible to spend a few quiet moments in contemplation or meditation.

In Chichen Itza, which is a popular tourist attraction in the Yucatán in Mexico, most people hover around the famous ancient Mayan pyramid, and the large open area surrounding it. But if you walk ten minutes away and visit the Sacred Cenote, you will find that the energies emanating from the ground there are far more powerful, and will appear if you spend a few minutes in appreciation of the gifts left to us by ancient peoples who had built a powerful civilization many years ago.

At the Taj Mahal, which is undoubtedly one of the most beautiful buildings in the world, the energy that is housed in the mosque on the left-hand side of the famous edifice is stronger than the energy emanating from the famous tomb. If you visit Agra on a day that is not a Friday (when the mosque is closed to visitors, but open to worshipers), you will be able to spend time in prayer and meditation at the mosque without being disturbed. You might also feel and appreciate the powerful energy that is housed in that beautiful building.

In St. Joseph's Cathedral in Montreal, the strongest energy is in the little chapel at the back where almost no one visits. This is the site where brother André built the original chapel dedicated to Saint Joseph with his own hands, and with the help of a friend. The original chapel was burnt down, but the energy is still there. Brother André was a known healer who through dedication and devotion connected to a natural healing energy that had lived in the mountain, and came to join his life at the beginning of the 20th century.

So if you want to connect to powerful high energies, move away from the noisy crowds, and look for out of the way places within ancient sites where powerful energies can reside in peace. Be quiet, be respectful, and hopefully you will be rewarded by being able to sense the very energies that had inspired the building of these ancient sites in the first place.

Express and Ingest

When we are pleased with ourselves, we tend to express it and share it. We like to accentuate what we think are our best features. For example, a woman puts on bright red lipstick when she is pleased with the shape of her mouth, or another woman wears a wide belt to accentuate a slim waist, or a girl wears her dresses short because she likes the shape of her legs.

The same tendency to share our strong qualities happens when we consider our skills and abilities. We go to college or university to advance the skills we believe we already have. If we are good at mathematics, we might study math; if we like to write, we might study English literature.

Conversely, we try to hide the aspects and features of ourselves that we do not like, or we think are weak. A woman might wear a long skirt to hide her bandy legs, or another woman might wear her hair long to cover up her ears that stick out from her head. Someone else might wear a cap to hide a balding head.

So we tend to express our strengths, because we exercise them daily. On the other hand, we tend to hide our weaknesses, and keep them locked inside. So we do not talk about them and keep them hidden, adding to the secret stash that builds up over time.

It is important to sometimes let our weaknesses out in safe circumstances, like when we laugh at a comedian expressing the very same weakness that we know we, too, have. We can also deliberately let them go by putting something better in their place. What we hide from view tends to grow, whereas flaws that are in plain sight can be laughed at, and their power can be thus reduced so that they cease to pose a threat to our self view.

It is important to know oneself, so that an unexpected burst of anger, or a bout of anxiety does not take us by surprise. When you know your weaknesses, you can work to eliminate them, by chipping away at them one step at a time. So, for example, a person who tends to be impatient might deliberately set out to be patient on a particular day, or someone who is stingy might deliberately decide to give something away on a regular basis. Thus we can take control of who we are and take steps to strengthen our character over time.

Homo Erectus

It must have been strange and completely new when the first Homo Erectus stood up.

He (or she) had been walking on all fours, but from time to time he would reach for a nut or a berry on a tree or bush and find that he could straighten up his legs and back, and reach higher and higher. Then one day, he thought to himself, "Maybe I can walk like this," and he took the first tenuous and hesitant step forward, with his head held high. One small step for him, but a great step for mankind. A new era was born that day.

The trouble began when he started walking in an upright position. Other humanoids saw him and immediately started berating him.

"Get down, get down," they cried. "You will hurt your back."

"You will cease up in that position and you will never be able to walk like us again!"

"It's not funny any more. We see you can clown around, but now get back down to our level!"

But he was a stubborn human and he liked to be able to see above the bushes, and spot the birds and the animals that dwelt within the foliage of the trees. Then a few of the younger humanoids saw him and decided to try it for themselves. And lo and behold, they, too, could walk upright. A new possibility had opened up in human affairs and the younger generation were seizing it.

"Look at us," they would say. "We are erect. We can use our hands for other things, rather than just walking. We can carry branches, leaves, and other building materials, and food. We feel free."

And slowly others joined the growing numbers of Homo Erectus. Within a couple of decades there were no more humanoids walking on all fours because evolution had given the human race their evolutionary next step.

Evolution is still in progress. What will be the next step for humankind to take?

The Sacred Is Everywhere

The sacred is everywhere. Reach out your hand and you are touching the sacred. "That is just air," you might say, but the air is sacred. Does it not sustain life and allow you to breathe in and replenish your lungs and feed your blood? "Every part of this Earth is sacred," Chief Seattle said.

Even on a busy city street one can be in touch with the sacred. All it takes is a moment of gratitude, a brief meditation, an act of kindness, or a prayer.

One day when I was living in Canada, I witnessed a sacred ceremony on a busy street in Toronto. My husband David and I had established a center for esoteric studies and personal development. We had acquired two large buildings in the heart of the city and I was busy purchasing fabric and sewing curtains at the time.

There was a great fabric store on College Street in the center of town and I used to frequently go there looking for affordable fabric and notions. At the entrance to the store there used to be a bin with bargains and remnants—pieces of material priced at a few dollars.

On this particular day I noticed a modestly dressed Native American woman rummaging through the bargain bin, until she found what she was looking for—a white piece of fabric with a pattern of small pink flowers, perhaps roses. She went inside the store and paid the cashier; when she came out onto the street, she had tied the fabric around her waist and she was wearing it like a skirt.

She then stood for a moment on the corner of the street and bowed to the four directions—the north, the east, the west, and the south—no doubt in gratitude for her purchase.

As she did this, it felt to me like time had stood still and everything went quiet—the noise of the traffic, the tram going by, the people hurrying on their way. I don't know if anyone else had noticed the little ceremony that occurred on a busy street in Toronto that day, but I felt the atmosphere change—there was something special in the air in response to the woman's giving of thanks.

I think gratitude is a gateway into the higher energy realms, as are joy, awe and inspiration. Moments when time seems to stand still are moments when we can connect to higher energies that can uplift our lives and heal our souls.

Change Your Vibration

Every person's energies vibrate at a certain level at any given time. There are feelings and character traits that cause lower vibrations, such as fear, jealousy, or greed. At a higher level there are qualities and virtues, such as patience, generosity, or gratitude.

As humans we have the ability to choose what level we want our energy field or aura to respond to. At any given moment we can decide to change our vibration, by thinking about higher energetic qualities, such as love, compassion, and care. These qualities will elevate one's energetic connections beyond the level of material possessions, and concerns about the physical worlds, into wonder about higher energetic realms, which are always there for us.

One way to do so is to consider what one is grateful for, and to create a list, beginning with the fact of being grateful for life itself. Then there are the people in one's life that we are grateful for, as well as all the rich inter-actions with these people, and the memories of special moments shared.

Connecting to nature is another way to increase one's vibration, because nature is tuned to the higher levels of the energy worlds. So a walk in a forest, or forest bathing as it is called in Japan, appreciating the beauty of the natural worlds, watching a beautiful sunset, or exploring the stars at night, are all effective ways to leave one's worries behind and connect to the healing energies the planet offers us in abundance.

Meditation is another well known method to change one's mental and emotional state. By observing one's breath, for example, one becomes anchored in the now, keeping at bay thoughts about the past, or worries about the future. The present moment is the only time when one can connect to higher energetic frequencies, so meditation is a good tool to start with.

Clairvoyance

When you look at something, you see it with your physical vision. You see it from your perspective, with your own bias, education, likes and dislikes, but you do see it, and nobody would dispute that you do. You trust your own eyes because you have had physical proof to confirm that what you have seen is really there.

With clairvoyance, results are not immediately seen or perceived. The word itself means "clear sight" and refers to the ability (which everyone has) to perceive the unseen, to detect frequency, and to simply know what lies beyond the material manifestation of something. So, clairvoyance is, for example, knowing what another person is thinking or feeling, knowing what will happen next, predicting the future, as well as reading the past.

Each person carries their history around with them in the form of electro-magnetic signals which are registered inside their aura. When your clairvoyant faculty switches on, you can know about another person without asking; you will sense and read their history, as well as their current thoughts and feelings. And just as each person carries around their history inside their aura, so does every building, place, site, street, district, and country have an astral light that is full of history, radiations, essences and influences.

Why do people in different parts of the world speak with different accents? Language is the *land-guage* and represents a read-out of the essences of the land. Thus, for example, people from the Southern States who speak with a southern drawl process a different kind of energy than, say, a New Yorker. Their speeds will be different and their way of thinking will be different; their behavior will be different as well. Try to speak slowly to a Northener and they will most probably become impatient. Try adopting a California attitude in Boston and see how far you get.

Clairvoyance is the ability to detect the radiation that emanates from the land, to recognize the features of a nation or place without previous knowledge or research. It is the ability to arrive in a country and to simply know what the prevailing energies of that part of the world are, so as to be able to adapt to the change of frequency and radiation, and to successfully communicate with the natives, without superimposing one's own customs or habits. It is difficult to change one's accent, but someone who is clairvoyant can soon appreciate the energetic nature of the place they are visiting.

Imagine going to the Taj Mahal, or walking into a room and knowing its history, as well as being able to pick up, like a receiving station, what had gone on in it in the last few hours, or days, or even longer. Perhaps one would then also be able to heal an atmosphere, and even out the ups and downs that might occur in a place in the course of a normal working day. Or one could detect a presence and help exorcise a bad feeling that lingers after an argument in a room or home, or perhaps even send a ghost back to where he or she had come from.

If people could learn clairvoyance as part of a natural education, the world would be a much more peaceful place, for we would understand each other better, rather than trying to enforce our own ways and customs on others who have different beliefs and traditions. We would know that each person is moved by a different set of essences and energies, and so, rather than judging another for being different, we might welcome the variety and acknowledge its potential as a learning opportunity.

Talent

Everyone has talents. Just as it is said in the biblical story in the New Testament, some people have more than others, but what matters is what you do with the talents you have been given, not whether you have one, five or ten.

One way to decide what your talents are is to look back upon your early lfe and see what you were able to do with little effort, much enjoyment, and great results. Whether it was a creative talent, like painting, singing or writing, or whether it was a way of communicating with others, or the art of persuasion, or whether you had a healing touch, does not matter. Every talent contributes to the wellbeing and inspiration of others.

Your talent might still be latent (which is an anagram of the word talent), but it is there, waiting to be discovered, brought out into the daylight and used. "Use it or lose it," the saying goes.

So in order to be the best person you can be, it is important to find your talent (or multiple talents) and put them to work, so other people can benefit from your unique skills and abilities.

The Knife Story

There once was a knife that lived in a drawer in a house that belonged to a family. The family consisted of Mr. and Mrs. Johnson and their three children: Mary who was the oldest, Eric and Andrew. The knife shared his drawer home with his cousins, the family cutlery—other knives, forks and spoons. The cutlery family was a proud lot; they considered themselves to be the silverware of the family and thought they were a cut above the ordinary implements which were housed in other drawers. They fulfilled their duties of serving, carrying and cutting with conscientiousness and reliability, except for one knife. This renegade implement had a certain peculiarity which was that he did not like to cut, no matter what he was called to dice, shred or chop. Whenever the cutlery drawer was opened and a hand reached into it to extract a knife, fork or spoon, this knife cowered in the corner of his compartment, praying that he would not be chosen to perform knife-cutting duties. Whenever one of the family members did manage to get hold of his handle, he would try to jump out of their hands, land with a bang on the floor, and be consequently placed in the dishwasher for a cleansing procedure. This he did not mind at all. "Better a bath than a cutting duty," he used to think to himself as he went through the washing cycle yet again.

One day Eric, who was seven-years-old at the time, was helping his mother lay the table and prepare for dinner.

The family were expecting a guest and had covered their dining room table with a white embroidered tablecloth, and the best china was brought out to honor the visitor. When Eric picked out six forks, he then reached for six knives, which was the entire contents of the knife compartment. Eric was holding the six knives in one hand and six forks in the other when one of the knives suddenly slipped out of his hand and slid under the fridge. Eric bent over to see if he could retrieve the knife from under the fridge, but he could not easily see it. So he decided to leave the recalcitrant knife where it lay and finished helping set up the table by omitting to put a knife alongside his own plate.

After the dinner all the dishes and cutlery were washed and put away, but the knife remained under the fridge because no one remembered he was there. It was dark and dusty under the fridge. At the beginning the knife was quite happy that he did not have to cut any-one's chicken or vegetables that evening, but after a whole night went by and in the morning he was still stuck under the fridge, he started to feel lonely. "No one cares that I am missing," he thought, as he longingly thought about his drawer home which he shared with the other knives. Next day came and went, and again no one noticed he was missing, as the family only needed five knives during their daily dinner time.

A whole week went by and the knife was feeling abandoned and miserable. He even started to wish that he was needed for cutting duty. "Anything would be better than lying in this dark hole," he thought. That evening Mary was helping set the table, and as she collected the soup spoons from the drawer, one of them fell close to the fridge. Mary took the rest of the spoons through to the dining room, as she intended to return and pick up the spoon she had dropped a moment later. In the meantime the spoon, from his vantage point on the floor, noticed the knife lying there in the dark under the fridge. The spoon inquired, "What are you doing there on your own? "

"I fell," the knife admitted. "I was hiding because I don't like to cut things, "he said.

"But you were made to cut and spread," the spoon replied. "You should be glad to do what you were made for," the spoon wisely added.

"You are right," the knife agreed, recognizing the error of his ways. "I should be glad to serve by fulfilling my purpose."

Following this brief exchange Mary returned to the kitchen, bent over to pick up the spoon she had dropped, and noticed the knife under the fridge. She retrieved both utensils, washed them and took them through to the dining room table.

"From now on I will be glad to do what I was made for," the knife announced to all who could hear him. All the other cutlery pieces cheered, for they had been worried that the knife was lost and were glad to see him returning to active duty.

Connection Is Possible

When there is a group, or a teacher who establishes an esoteric school, and attracts a number of students who are responding to the atmosphere of the place, and the promise of personal development—they are feeling the elevation brought about by that teacher, and it belongs to the teacher, not the students. The moment the students leave the cover of the school, they are subject to the level of their own development, and unless they make that elevation their own through application and work, they will lose it, because it was not theirs in the first place. It is for the student to do the work of personal development on their own to make it become part of their life and their endeavor.

The benefit of having been in such a school with real connections to the Host is knowing that it exists and that living an enhanced life is possible. Having experienced an enhanced atmosphere, it can alter one's life, so one will be forever seeking to repeat the experience, whether inside the school walls or within one's own life.